D1514715

URBAN PAPER

HOW
BOOKS
Cincinnati, Ohio
www.howdesign.com

URBAN PAPER

26 designer toys to cut out and build

MATT HAWKINS

For more resources for designers, visit www.howdesign.com.

13 12 11 10 09   5 4 3 2 1

Distributed in Canada by Fraser Direct
100 Armstrong Avenue
Georgetown, Ontario, Canada L7G 5S4
Tel: (905) 877-4411

Distributed in the U.K. and Europe by David & Charles
Brunel House, Newton Abbot, Devon, TQ12 4PU, England
Tel: (+44) 1626-323200, Fax: (+44) 1626-323319
E-mail: postmaster@davidandcharles.co.uk

Distributed in Australia by Capricorn Link
P.O. Box 704, Windsor, NSW 2756 Australia
Tel: (02) 4577-3555

Library of Congress Cataloging-in-Publication Data

Hawkins, Matt.
  Urban paper : 26 designer toys to cut out and build /
Matt Hawkins. -- 1st ed.
       p. cm.
  Includes bibliographical references and index.
  ISBN 978-1-60061-123-0 (pbk. : alk. paper)
  1. Paper work. 2. Toy making. I. Title.
  TT870.H38135 2009
  745.592--dc22
                              2008051648

Edited by Amy Schell
Designed by Grace Ring
Production coordinated by Greg Nock

DEDICATION

Dedicated to Alicia, my inspiration.

ACKNOWLEDGMENTS

Thanks to all the artists featured in this book who so graciously gave their time and talent to make this book possible.

Thanks to my editor, Amy Schell, for all her help and understanding.

Thanks to Jaime Zollars at Paper Forest for sharing her paper passion and inspiring me to take up papertoy design.

Thanks to Nate Soria for all his help with the slideshow and DVD material.

Thanks to Lismore for the killer music tracks for the slide show on the DVD.

Thanks to all the folks who visit my blog and download my toys and send me pics and keep me going.

Thanks to all the talented folks at C3, who keep me inspired on a daily basis and help me out when I come in all sleep-deprived and groggy.

Thanks to my twin brother, Ben, for sharing his creativity and passion.

And finally, a special thanks to my family—Alicia, Henry and Lily—for helping me, inspiring me and making every day the best one ever.

ABOUT THE AUTHOR

Matt Hawkins is an incessant doodler. He lives in Kansas City with Alicia, Henry and Lily. By day, he works at C3, a children's marketing agency, as an illustrator/papertoy designer. By night he stays up way too late in his attic studio making designer papertoys for his own amusement and freelance papertoys for clients. He shares his papertoys with the world at www.custompapertoys.com. He's always cutting or folding or gluing something.

WITHDRAWN

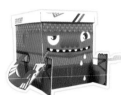

TABLE OF CONTENTS

FOREWORD

For the uninitiated, mention the term "papertoy" and you may conjure up childhood memories of an airplane folded out of torn blue-lined notebook paper, gliding silently through the air…or a paper boat fashioned from a magazine spread, frantically bobbing up and down on a flooded canal…or even that time you charmed your friend with a single paper crane, or a hundred or so…OK, maybe the last memory was from a sappy telefeature.

My personal experience with papertoys is categorized simply into "pre-blog" and "post-blog" eras.

All above regaled memories and impressions were prior to my path down blogdom (i.e., pre-blog). They focused primarily on simple origami constructs of both inanimate objects and animals, a simple and effective play of both form manipulation and physics. But "designer papertoys" may encompass all that and more, including giving "character" and perhaps even "life" to the construct by popping out at you via two-dimensional form, be it on printed paper or through the computer screen.

Then, when I first logged online, I was drawn into a diverse world of the fantastic.

I devoured paper crafts online—from the amazing precision and technicality of Pepakura Designer, to the wondrous mechanics of paper automata—but nothing rang as inspired and as true as designer papertoys. Most of them were constructs and creations of designers of the vector realms, three-dimensional shapes and characters created out of the two-dimensional vectors, challenging perceptions of the craft. What I find most appealing is the ability of their creations to cross over with other fellow designers—for collaborations and a general sharing within the papertoy community. That, to me, is the "spirit" of this art form and pop-cultural design movement, still awaiting its due and recognition amongst the masses.

From beyond the cyber-pixelled highway, you now have in your hands a collection of the cream of the crop papersmiths and designers. They have held my attention and wonder over the years that I've had the privilege and honor of featuring them on my blog. This is a collection of not just awesome designs on paper, but also of like-minded professionals and enthusiasts who share with you their creations and designs, and who perhaps may inspire you toward your own creations.

Meanwhile, sharpen those scissors, ready the glue and prepare yourself to re-enter the world of innocence past, with a design eye focused on the now and an imagination primed for the flip of the page toward the future.

Your humble papertoy enthusiast,

ANDY HENG
toysrevil.net

INTRODUCTION

The online papertoy phenomenon is like a matter transporter. An artist creates a 3-D object, it is flattened out and sent through cyberspace as a bunch of ones and zeros, and then reassembled as a 3-D object half a world away. That's just one of the things I love about papertoys!

There seems to be an explosion of late of free online designer papertoys. It's the rage of the age. Lots of artists and designers are taking the traditional art of paper craft and making it their own. What was once a landscape of scale model cars, geometric shapes and anime robots has become a fertile stomping ground for urban and lowbrow artists.

I first discovered the world of papertoys while surfing the net for inspiration (i.e., procrastinating) when I came across the Paper Forest blog (www.paperforest.blogspot.com). There, I found so many fun little paper crafts to download, print, cut and glue. I was instantly fascinated by these cool 3-D objects that were born of flat pieces of paper. Magic! I started searching all over the web for paper crafts. I was amazed at the thousands of free downloads to be found. Within a couple of weeks, my cubicle was filled with little papertoys. Japanese robots, anime and video game characters, Readymechs and Spiky Babies. I found a lot of papertoys that were just as well designed, if not better, as any "designer" vinyl toy.

Many good toner cartridges were laid to waste.

This was not only a more budget-friendly way to collect cool toys from great designers, but also an opportunity for me to make and distribute my own line of designer toys.

Papertoys take the whole designer toy phenomenon and make it a little more DIY, grassroots and inclusive. What could be more available, inexpensive and environmentally friendly than paper?

Paper breaks down a lot of the barriers that would otherwise keep an artist from making a toy. It gets rid of the cost restrictions for both the artist and the fan, distribution can be anywhere in the world and the supply is practically unlimited. Imagine it: anyone with an Internet connection, a printer and an hour to waste could own one of your toys.

You don't have to have a big company, a factory in China or a lot of money behind you to create and share a papertoy with the people who enjoy your work. Your distribution is anywhere in the world that has an Internet connection. My toys are in places and built by people I never would have reached with a $40 vinyl toy.

With all the barriers that papertoys tear down for a designer, a papertoy can be a much more personal and unique form of creative expression. No one is hanging over you telling you this won't sell or that won't sell, do it this way or that. The only restraint is your own imagination. And with a global distribution, your work will be found by the people who will enjoy it.

Papertoys are participatory in a way that a lot of creative outlets are not. I love the fact that it requires participation from the user to bring a papertoy to life. There is a bond with a papertoy that you helped realize, which isn't there with something you buy at a store and put on a shelf. You invest a little of yourself every time you build a papertoy.

Another cool thing about papertoys is they make great "platform toys." Digital files can be shared and customized by other designers. Some of the designers in this book have included blank templates on the DVD-ROM so you can customize your own version of their toys. You could have hundreds of custom toys by hundreds of artists available to the public.

I think, though, that my favorite thing about papertoys is that you can create the entire project yourself. Every little detail is yours to create; you don't have to rely on turnaround drawings and sculptors and manufacturing plants to get your ideas across. Imagine starting out with a sketch, and within a couple hours, holding the final product in your hands and distributing it worldwide. The sky is the limit.

It's just paper. The only real value papertoys have is the joy the designer gets out of designing and sharing it, and the joy the builder gets out of gluing it together and setting it on his desk. None of this collecting it because it will be worth something someday stuff. Paper lets you get past the whole consumer/collector thing and just share art.

The first papertoy I designed was a character from a comic book project I had just finished. I was instantly hooked. A couple months later, I started up the Custom Paper Toys blog (www.custompapertoys.com) as a place to share all the papertoys I was making. It has been such a joy sharing my work with others who enjoy it. I also joined the crew at the Paper Forest blog so I could share with others all the cool papertoys—especially the cool urban and designer papertoys—I was discover-

ing. It seemed like every time I turned around, there was a new papertoy project.

I guess it's kind of a strange idea to try to capture a quick-moving, free Internet phenomenon in a book. I just wanted to share with you some of my favorite paper designers, talented folks from every corner of the globe, give some insight into their work and showcase their amazing toys all in one place. I also hope to inspire you to create your own little pulpy friend with some of the tricks and tips on papertoy design featured in this book. Not to mention offer you some exclusive papertoys you can't find anywhere else.

In the front of this book, you'll find a little tutorial for designing papertoys that is a culmination of my own experiences and those of the other designers I've interviewed. The rest of the book contains interviews and papertoys by some of the best papertoy designers around. On the DVD-ROM that is included, you'll find digital files of the toys featured in this book, which you can print and build if you don't want to cut up your book. There are also some blank templates you can customize, and other cool surprises.

I mean, where else can you get more than two dozen designer toys for the price of a book and a little glue, huh?

Paper to the people,

MATT HAWKINS
2008

ALL ABOUT PAPERTOYS

HOW TO DESIGN YOUR OWN PAPERTOY

So, you want to design your own papertoy, but you're not a paper engineer with a doctorate in geometry? No worries; this section of the book is full of tips and tricks on papertoy designing from me and other papertoy designers to help you get going. Your shapes don't have to be complicated to make a killer papertoy; the effect is in how you apply them creatively. In fact, the simpler you can keep it, the easier it will be to build and the more people will download it and actually build it. Some of the most popular papertoys are the simplest. My most downloaded papertoys are the Tri-Bunnies, and they are by far my simplest design.

My first piece of advice on designing your own papertoy is to build a few papertoys that were designed by other artists to see how it's done. The amazing toys in this book would be a great place to start. This will give you a basic idea of how 3-D shapes can be formed from the flat page, and will inspire you to come up with your own applications for these ideas. Keep an inventory of things that you think are clever and well executed about a toy, as well as the things that aren't so, um, desirable. These will be good things to keep in mind as you design your own toy. Take into consideration that your toy will have to be built by someone else, and you that want that to be a satisfying experience. So building up a few papertoys will help put you in their shoes.

Another great way to get your paper feet wet is to design a custom papertoy on a blank template from another designer. Many papertoy designers offer blank templates of their toys that you can add your own art and design "skin" to. This is a great little baby step toward designing your own form. Once you see your artwork come to life in 3-D, you'll be hooked! Lots of artists, like Ben the Illustrator, even release custom collaborations on their websites, so you could be part of their custom series. There are a few of these blank DIY papertoys available on this book's DVD-ROM for you to go nuts on. If you do a custom of another designer's papertoy, be sure to give credit where credit is due, and don't release the design to the public until you have received permission from the original template designer.

Note: This is a problem that is particular to papertoys, because if an artist distributes his work for free, people think it's free for the pilfering. Plus, most artists release their work as PDF or Illustrator files, so it can be tempting to just "Command-C" something from someone else's toy. One of the great benefits of working with papertoys is the collaboration and sharing between designers. But believe me, these things we distribute freely mean as much to us as something we would charge money for. When in doubt, just check with the original designer. I've included a few basic shapes templates on the DVD-ROM. Please feel free to cut and paste and use these any way you'd like to.

Inspired and ready to create your own unique papertoy design?

Here are a few ideas on concepting for paper as well as creating your toy's template. I'll show you step by step how I created the papertoy for this book, Oliver Ollie, as well as share some tips and insight from other designers on their papertoy processes.

CONCEPTING A PAPERTOY

It all starts with the character or concept. What are you gonna make? It takes a considerable amount of time and effort to design a papertoy, and if you're going to invest all that, you want to make sure what you're creating is going to be totally sweet. Chances are, if you are reading this section of the book anyway, you already have some sort of an idea you'd like to see in your papertoy. Ultimately, it will be the character of your toy that will inspire another person to download it and build it.

Concepting for a papertoy is unique, with many unique challenges. There are several ways of going about concepting a papertoy and coming up with that killer idea. You can start with a sketch, some dimensional doodling, a basic shape or a previously designed character. There is no one right way of doing it; most designers I interviewed use some combination of these concepting techniques. I have used them all at one time or another.

Most of the time, I start with a sketch or a doodle. I'm an incessant doodler and keep a doodle log, which is always a great place for me look for a new toy idea. When you're sketching, keep in mind that you are designing a three-dimensional character, not a two-dimensional one. Sketch in geometric shapes and plains. Since I usually end up doing most of my papertoy work digitally, I like to keep my sketches pretty loose at this point. I find that if I do a really tight sketch, my work on the computer can get a little

stiff. Instead, I keep the sketches loose, so when I start working on the computer, I'm still searching and creating excitement, as opposed to just rendering something as faithfully as possible. That way, even the technical parts become points of creative discovery. I always try to use recycled paper, and I sometimes end up doodling and sketching on whatever I can find. Nothing is as creatively void to me as a clean, white, crisp piece of paper. Now, the piece of paper that I printed MapQuest directions to Columbus, Ohio, on last weekend and that has been blowing around my backseat ever since, that piece of paper has some history and is filled with creative energy. That's where I'm sketching.

Dimensional doodling is another great way to concept a character for a papertoy. Take some scrap paper and start folding and gluing and cutting and bending shapes. You'll begin to see cool forms and ideas that can inspire your papertoy concept. I like this method because you actually start with paper from the get-go. You'll come across much more interesting and organic shapes this way than by creating cubes and right angles on a computer. As you glue and cut and tape and re-cut, you can start to develop a really rough and ugly prototype that can then be disassembled and flattened out. You can then scan these flat shapes into a program like Adobe Illustrator and draw on top of them. You can use your digital tools to get all the angles and lengths right, giving you a great base for developing a template.

Chicken scratch, or America's next million-dollar papertoy design? This is the doodle log that contained the doodle that inspired my toy. Next to that are the loose sketches I did that start breaking down the form into geometric shapes.

Sometimes I find that as I'm working on a papertoy, a form emerges that will inspire an idea for a new form or shape, or the next evolution of that form. I'll build this shape blank and turn it around, set it upside down and look at it from all angles, and that may inspire a papertoy. Sometimes I'll just build a lot of experimental shapes and play with them and mix and match them, and a toy may be inspired. The same can be done with simple shapes like cubes and pyramids. On the DVD-ROM, I have included some basic shape templates you can use as a jumping-off point.

I take a similar approach when designing a custom of someone else's papertoy. I'll print out a blank template and look at it from every angle until it inspires an idea.

Or you may want to create a papertoy of a character that already exists. This is one of the more challenging ways to create a papertoy because the character wasn't designed with the limits of paper in mind. These usually turn out to be more complex models if you try to get the character exactly. You might want to consider "papertoy-ifying" your design and simplify your character into a few basic geometric shapes. Sometimes it looks really cool and iconic and kawaii to simplify a character down into a few basic forms

CREATING A TEMPLATE

Once you have a character in mind and a rough idea for its form, the next step is to create the template for your toy. There are two ways I know to do this: (1) use a 3-D modeling program and a program like Pepakura Designer, or (2) use a trial-and-error method in a program like Adobe Illustrator. I, and most of the designers I interviewed for this book, prefer to use the latter method.

Pepakura Designer (www.tamasoft.co.jp/pepakura-en) is a shareware program that can take the information from a model made in a 3-D modeling program, like Google SketchUp, and unfold it into a 2-D paper craft. The program basically takes the polygon information in the 3-D model and flattens it out. So the template you get could be made of hundreds of tiny little folds and glue points; it just depends on how complicated the 3-D model is. To a novice paper craft fan, a complicated paper model can seem intimidating to build. Since the software doesn't think about how difficult or easy something is to build, some models it renders can be humanly impossible to build. Every form made in this program uses only flat polygons, so there are no graceful, fold-less curves calculated by the program. Seemingly round shapes are actually made of a ton of polygons, which makes the model a mess of folds and cuts. I can tell you from experience that there is nothing more frus-

Masking tape mummy. This is the humble beginnings of the mighty Grumm papertoy by Matthijs Kamstra. It's like a dimensional rough sketch.

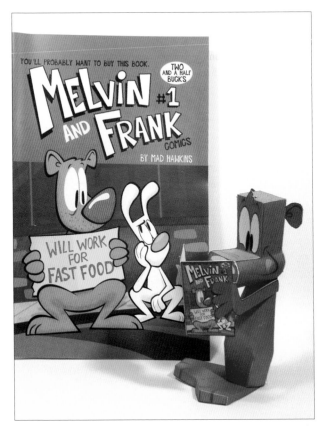

Ripped right out of the funny pages. Here is a papertoy I created based on an established character. I had to make some shapes more geometric and angular to translate Melvin from the comic page to a papertoy.

Island of misfit papertoys. I go through many revisions of each papertoy I create. Here are but a few of the warped and twisted corpses of not-quite-there-yets.

trating than spending hours building a paper model that was made by this program and getting to the last piece, only to find no physical way of getting it in place. The program also tends to separate things that could easily be made out of one piece and create simple shapes in a complex, unnatural way. Models made with this method look pretty amazing with an insane level of detail. I'm not knocking this software. I just think this route is better suited for people who want to make super-detailed paper replicas of the *Millennium Falcon* rather than for folks who want to make cool, easy-to-build paper models.

The method I use, and that most of the designers in this book use, is a trial-and-error process. This takes a little bit of patience—OK, a lot of patience. With this method, I'm playing with math that I don't quite understand, so I need to build and rebuild and try different things. This is where the patience comes in. Depending on how complicated the toy is, it can take quite a few revisions to get the template just right.

Here is a step-by-step explanation of the process—actually, the one I used to create Oliver Ollie for this book.

After I have the rough sketches, I start designing flat in Adobe Illustrator. I use Illustrator to design templates because of the flexibility the program gives to change the template a little this way or that. Vector art is pretty elastic.

I first start out by making shapes I think will work, based on my initial sketch. I begin with the major forms of the body.

I use a fold instead of a glue joint whenever I can because it makes the model easier to build, and it takes up less space on the template sheet. The built toy will also be more sturdy if there are folds instead of glue joints. Trying to make as few separate pieces as possible is one of my goals at this early stage.

I also try to keep my toys to one page, if possible, in order to save the builder some paper and toner. However, I want the toy to be as big as possible to aid construction. It can become quite the Tetris game, arranging and rearranging to find the best way to fit all the pieces on one sheet of paper!

I like to leave the bottom of the toy open when possible. This helps make it easier to build, and it will stand easier and use less space on your page. No use wasting space and time on something no one will see.

I know I will need to make changes to my template several times, and I don't want to have to move or redraw a lot of details. I like to rough in the major details and start placing colors from the get-go. When I do create the details, I have them go across several different panels of the shape to give a more organic flow, which helps it look less geometric and stiff. I feel the form and the "skin," or art on the template, are of equal importance, so I like to develop them together in service of one another.

At this point, I don't do anything for the details like arms and legs. I'm just trying to flesh out the main structure of the toy.

Best guess. This is my first shot at the template flat in Adobe Illustrator. Just trying to rough in the main shapes, the body and the head.

Ya gotta start somewhere. This is the first of many dimensional builds I will make bringing little Oliver Ollie into the world. This gives me something to work with.

I don't worry about drawing glue tabs and dotting the fold lines yet. The template will be moved and reshaped a lot, so there's no reason to draw and redraw a lot of unnecessary stuff in the beginning stages.

Once I have the basic shapes and art roughed in, I print out the template and build it. I usually hand draw tabs on the print so it can go together quickly, but if I can just slop a big piece of tape on it to hold it together, I will. It doesn't have to look pretty; it's just for getting something dimensional to build on.

Once this rough draft is constructed, I see what changes I need to make (and there are usually a ton in this first round), and I go back to my template.

Before I start to monkey with the file, I re-save the file as version 1, 2, 3, etc. Sometimes you'll put a lot of work into changing something, and then realize you liked it better the first time. Save a new file each time, because it's easier than maniacally hitting Command-Z and praying that you don't run out of steps backward before you get it back where you want it.

Thus begins the trial and error. I make changes, print, build, make changes, print, build.

On the second round, I start committing to basic forms, developing the supporting details, like arms and legs, and filling in more detail on pieces I feel pretty good about. I try to contrast round forms with sharp forms, and I try to get away from being super symmetrical, which is a tendency many designers have when working with geometric shapes.

Remember that not every piece has to be dimensional. I often do arms as a solid, flat piece. I also like to do the front and back of these pieces so they can be glued together and don't appear blank on one side. This also makes these pieces a little sturdier.

As the template gets more refined, I add in more and more of the details so that as the revisions go on, I'm not only getting the template correct, I'm also figuring out where the final art is going to be to best develop the personality and look of the character. As soon as I get a part of the model right, I might start doing the finished art on that piece, even before the rest of the template is finalized. Doing all the technical template stuff can get tiresome, so it's nice to flip back and forth between the creative and the technical, or maybe it's just my adult ADD kickin' in. Doing the art as I go along also helps keep me inspired to see a part as it will look done, which encourages me to finish the rest.

As I go through all these revisions, I pay close attention to where I draw on the glue tabs. I usually change it up from prototype to prototype to see what looks best and what is easiest to assemble. As I get closer to the final version, I actually put the glue tabs on the template. By doing this, I can make sure everything fits together and no tabs overlap slots.

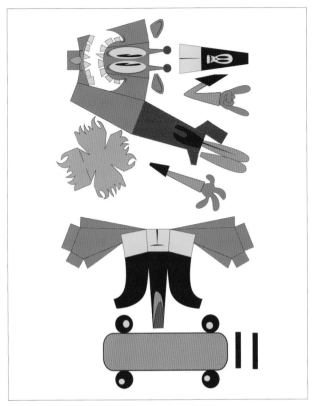

Round two. Here is the second round of changes to the template. It's getting more complex and will need two pages. I'm starting to rough in more detail in the parts I feel good about.

Gettin' there, Gettin' there. Here is round four of revisions built. Just need to make a few more revisions to the feet so he'll stand on his skateboard, but he's pretty darn close at this point.

A few things to think about when making glue tabs are the size, shape, placement and number of tabs.

You want to make sure a tab is big enough to get glue on, because tiny tabs can be irritating to work with. Try to taper your tabs instead of doing them totally square; this will help keep tabs from gluing on top of joints, and it will allow the panels of the shape to fit together snuggly. Place a tab along a long, straight piece if you can. When going around a curve, you don't have to put in a ton of tiny little flaps. Sometimes one or two tabs is enough because the paper will naturally bend and flow from one tab to the next. Some small curves don't need any tabs at all because the paper will naturally bend from one flat tab to the next flat tab. When using tabs to close a shape like a cube, put two tabs on the sides of the cube and one on the "lid," like a box; this will make the form tight and easy to seal.

Once I'm completely satisfied with the form and the roughed-in art, I can go nuts with all the final designing and art. I might build the form once or twice through this phase, too, just to make sure everything is working and looking the way I want it to. Be aware as you design that these templates will be printed on a home printer. Extensive background design and multiple pages can really suck a printer cartridge dry.

This is the fun part. But the next part isn't so fun.

PREPARING YOUR PAPERTOY FOR DOWNLOAD AND WRITING INSTRUCTIONS

Once every little thing is done in the design, the last thing I do in my process is make the cut and fold lines and write the instructions. These are both kinda tedious and not very creative, but you've worked so hard designing your toy, you can't give up now!

There is no set standard for designating cut and fold lines. I like to use solid lines for the cut lines and a dashed line for the folds; some folks like it the other way around. I personally like to do the fold lines as dashed because the fold lines will be visible on the final model, and a dashed line is a little softer on the eye. Some folks even like to designate between mountain folds and valley folds—anything that makes assembly easier. This is where working in Adobe Illustrator comes in handy. In the program, I use the direct selection tool to click on the side of a shape copy and past in front and then turn that line into a dashed line or a solid line. You might consider making these lines out of a darker hue of the color they're against, instead of making them all black; it makes the lines a little less noticeable on the final built toy. Something else to keep in mind is the thickness of your cut and fold lines. If the lines become too thick, the person assembling the toy won't know whether to cut to the inside or outside of the line or down the middle; this can make a finished toy look a bit sloppy.

I think writing clear and concise instructions for the assembly of papertoys is one place that a lot of papertoy designers drop the ball. This is probably because it's the least fun part of the process, but there's nothing worse than seeing one of your toys show up online that has been built wrong and looks all nasty. You'll think, "What have those monsters done to my little baby?" This might happen no matter how good your instructions are, but you should try to give people every chance you can to actually do it right. I feel that if people download my toy and they are going to spend the time to bring the little dude to life, I at least owe it to them to make the toy as easy to assemble as possible.

In the trial-and-error process, you've already built your toy a few hundred times, so who would know better than you how to write clear instructions of how to get it together? I prefer to write step-by-step instructions, and sometimes I'll even number the tabs to show what order they go together easiest in.

And then all I do is save it as a PDF, and she's ready to go! Note: Some people like to "password protect" their PDF files from being editable. You can find this option in the "Save as PDF" pop up.

Now your papertoy is ready for its debut on the World Wide Web. If you don't have a lot of bandwidth to play with, there are several free file hosting sites you can use to store your files. My personal favorite is Mediafire (www.mediafire.com). That way, you can share your toys for free without getting hit with bandwidth fees. You might also want to share your work with other papertoy enthusiasts/geeks at papertoy web communities like Nice Papertoys (www.nicepapertoys.com).

HOW TO BUILD THE MODELS IN THIS BOOK

Every model in this book is as unique as the artist who created it. While each one will have its own particular instructions, here are some basic how-tos for building papertoys.

What you will need:

Paper

If you are going to print the papertoys from the DVD-ROM instead of carving up the book, I recommend card stock or a thick, matte photo paper. I like the thickness of card stock, but I find that on most home ink-jet printers, the colors will look much better on a matte photo paper. Some of the coated card stocks can get a little too slick for glue. Glue adheres best to a matte finish.

Cutting Tools

I would definitely recommend a good, sharp craft knife (such as an X-Acto knife) instead of a pair of scissors for cutting out the toys in this book. Running a craft knife down a straight edge is a great way to get a clean, precise edge. It's also easier to get all the little details cut right without ripping the paper. Freehanding with scissors can rip and bend the paper. A good cutting mat also helps a great deal.

Adhesives

I personally recommend glue over double-sided tape. Tape is much faster and cleaner, but it doesn't seem to hold up over time—it starts to pop off. A white glue like Elmer's is a good choice because it dries quick and clear (sort of), and it holds up over time. Some of the "tacky" glues work great, too.

Tweezers

If you have fat or clumsy fingers, a good pair of tweezers can go a long way to achieving a good-looking papertoy.

Building the Toys

After you rip out a page from the book or print a papertoy from the DVD-ROM, the first thing to do is score the fold lines. Scoring the fold lines will give you crisp and accurate folds that will help your toy go together better and look nicer. Scoring can be done in several different ways. My preferred method is to very lightly run a sharp craft knife down the straight edges. You want to just barely break the top layer of the paper, not cut all the way through. You can also use a dead ballpoint pen. I find a Micron or a pen with a fine tip works fairly well. As a last resort, you can straighten out a paper clip and run the end down the straight edges. Try to keep the paper clip fairly tilted down because if it's too perpendicular, it will catch and rip the paper.

Next, cut out all the parts with your craft knife. If you are patient enough, use a straight edge as you do this to get the straight cuts perfect.

As you start to glue the pieces together, try to use a very thin and even application of glue. This way, the glue will dry faster, and less of it will squeeze out of the joint. You also want to avoid the paper getting too wet with the glue because it will cause warping and discoloring. Try to keep your fingers free of glue. Nothing looks worse than a few gnarly glue boogers on your papertoy. This is where a pair of tweezers comes in handy.

If you're super hardcore, once you're done assembling the toy, break out the Prismacolors and touch up the white flash that happens at the folds.

Happy papertoy making!

OLIVER OLLIE

by Matt Hawkins
Kansas City, Missouri, USA

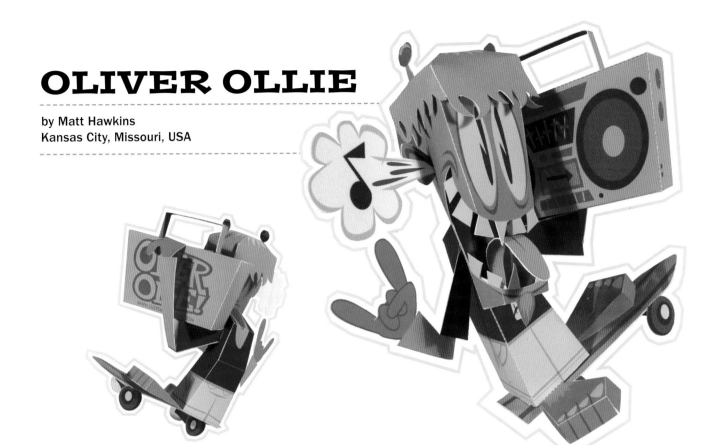

1. Prescore all dotted fold lines by gently running a craft knife down a straight edge.

2. Cut out all objects. Be sure to cut the ANTENNA slots in the HAIR, the HANDLE slots in the top of the GHETTO BLASTER, the EAR slots in the sides of the HEAD, the two slots in the top of the SKATEBOARD, the three ARM slots in the sides of the BODY and around the bottom of his GOATEE.

3. Start with the MELON. Fold and glue his ANTENNA front to back. Glue tabs A and B inside to the back of MELON. Glue tabs C to close bottom of MELON.

4. Fold the TONGUE and glue front to back.

5. Gently bend inside of mouth and slide inside MELON so inside of mouth is covered.

6. To form HAIR glue tabs A then tabs B. Insert ANTENNA through slots in HAIR and slide it down over MELON.

7. Fold and glue EARS front to back and insert into MELON.

8. Next build GHETTO BLASTER. First fold and glue GHETTO BLASTER HANDLE front to back. Do not glue white tabs on ends of HANDLE together.

9. Fold HANDLE into a U shape and insert tabs into slots on top of GHETTO BLASTER and glue tabs to inside.

10. Glue tabs A-D to finish GHETTO BLASTER.

11. Next build the BODY. Glue tabs A and B to inside of BODY FRONT. Glue tabs C to back of BODY. Glue tabs D to BODY FRONT. Glue tabs E to sides of BODY to finish.

12. Glue green tabs on top end of BODY to the light green areas on MELON.

13. Fold and glue RIGHT ARM, front to back, and insert into single slot on right side of BODY.

14. Glue white tab on LEFT ARM to form upper ARM. Fold and glue lower ARM front to back. Insert LEFT ARM into slots on BODY. Make sure the words "GLUE BLASTER HERE!" are on the top side of ARM.

15. Glue GHETTO BLASTER to arm where it's marked by lighter colors. GLUE left HAND to top of GHETTO BLASTER where marked.

16. Next build SKATEBOARD. Fold TRUCKS in half. Glue dark purple parts of TRUCKS front to back. Make sure you don't glue the pink parts or the little dark purple tabs on the ends together.

17. Glue TRUCKS to bottom of SKATEBOARD where marked.

18. Insert tabs F of BODY into slots on SKATEBOARD so his left foot is parallel to SKATEBOARD. Fold out tabs F and glue to inside SKATEBOARD.

19. Fold and glue SKATEBOARD, top to bottom.

20. Fold WHEELS down and glue to dark purple tabs on the end of TRUCKS.

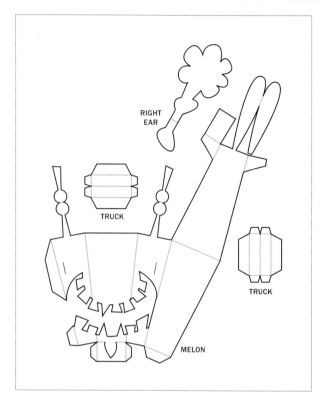

RIGHT EAR

TRUCK

TRUCK

MELON

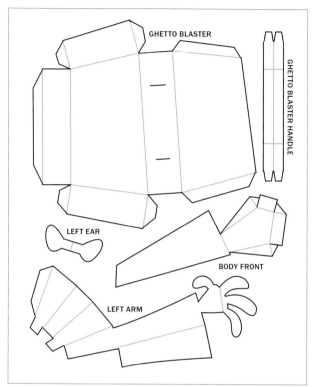

GHETTO BLASTER

GHETTO BLASTER HANDLE

LEFT EAR

BODY FRONT

LEFT ARM

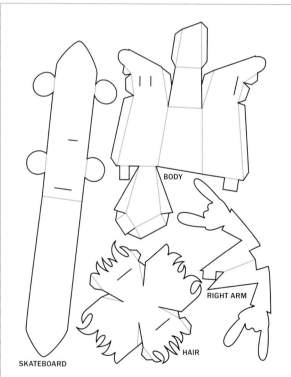

BODY

RIGHT ARM

SKATEBOARD

HAIR

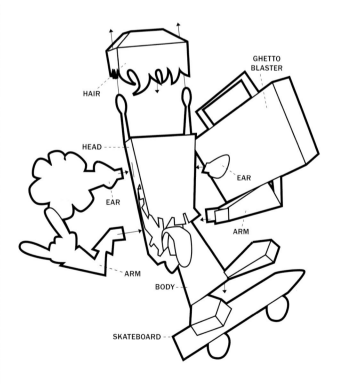

HAIR

HEAD

EAR

EAR

ARM

ARM

BODY

SKATEBOARD

GHETTO BLASTER

GHETTO BLASTER

GHETTO BLASTER HANDLE

WWW.CUSTOMPAPERTOYS.COM

GLUE ARM HERE!

GLUE LEFT HAND HERE!

GLUE "BLASTER" HERE!

LEFT EAR

BODY FRONT

LEFT ARM

No. 1 **NO ANCHOVIES ANDY**

by LouLou
Tilburg, The Netherlands

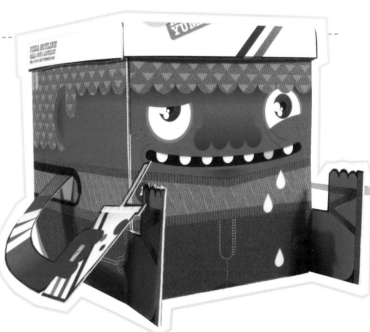

So what was it that drew you to designing papertoys?

About nine or ten years ago, a friend showed me some *Acme Novelty Library Comics* by Chris Ware. One of my favorite things in there were his awesome paper crafts. I guess that was the first time the idea of making cool paper crafts was planted in my head.

A few years later at the art academy (St. Joost in Breda, The Netherlands), we got the assignment to design a free giveaway game or toy for kids. Inspired by Chris Ware and the many Japanese paper crafts I could find on the Internet, I came up with a paper craft character on a surfboard that could wobble on a spring from a ballpoint. Very nifty. You can still download it from my site (www.loulouandtummie.com), by the way. I really had a lot of fun creating it, and it made me want to do more.

I've really enjoyed your square fruit series. They are easy to build and loaded with character. Are you planning on doing more of those? How did you come about doing these for *Cutie* magazine?

Thank you. When I started sketching, I had big plans: cubic carrots, lemons, strawberries and even a cluster of grapes, and also vegetables like tomatoes and leek. I saw it all before me, all different stackable characters. It was going to be the paper craft project of the year! I was creating them for the "fruit and vegetable" issue of *Cutie* (www.cutiemagazine.nl), a Dutch comic webzine by some befriended comic artists. I had the sketches lying around for months but, as it often goes with

unpaid submissions, I ended up creating only two of the fruits just one day before the deadline. So, perhaps I will do one more someday (I really liked the leek character sketch), but I usually tend to do something different each time.

So what projects, paper or non-paper, are you working on now? What's in store for all the LouLou fans out there?

The last few months, I have been very busy with my illustration work, so there will be a lot of magazines, posters, campaigns, books and such coming featuring my work. And I have teamed up with my girlfriend, Tummie—who is a designer, too—so we can do bigger and more diverse projects together.

One of the fun jobs I am currently working on is an interior design project. Together with graphic designer FormAddict, interior designers Workshop of Wonders and my agency, ShopAround, we created big wall designs that will be splattered over the walls, floor and ceiling, combined with a super fun interior. A little while ago, Tummie and I were asked to do another wall design, and I hope to do more of these projects in the near future.

With all that stuff on your plate and more coming, how do you stay inspired?

It sounds like a stupid cliché, but inspiration is really everywhere. Everything I see can inspire me, especially when I'm in a creative mood.

I love retro stuff, old movie posters and food labels. Spending time at secondhand markets collecting toys and robots, found photos, test and sound-effect records, and all sorts of other junk inspires me for sure. There is a lot of great packaging and record sleeves to be found. I also really enjoy looking at maps, constructions, machines and buildings.

Do you collect any toys yourself? Paper, designer, or otherwise?

Oh, yes, I certainly do. I love toys, always did. I remember once when I was about sixteen years old, a friend of mine said, "Dude, you've got to get rid of all those robots and stuff in your room. It really doesn't look mature. You'll never score chicks this way."

I started collecting robots when I was about that age. My collection isn't really special, I'm not picky about what I buy. I don't have a lot of collector's items, NRFB (Never Removed From Box), mint conditions or whatever. It's all for fun. When I grew a little older, I also started buying the McFarlane comic action figures and stuff. And I started regretting ever selling all my He-Man, G.I. Joe and Mask figures, so I started buying all that stuff again, too, at secondhand markets.

Now, with all the designer toys out there, my collection is expanding rapidly. I buy and order designer toys that I like every once in a while. But have to say that 99 percent of all the "designer" toys are crap, especially now there is so much coming out every month.

I don't care if it is designer, new, old or whatever kind of toy. I just buy what I like. But I do have a thing for plastic robots; I hardly have any tin robots. I download a paper craft toy once in a while, but I prefer designing them, not actually making them. I only print and make the simple ones. I still often go to second-hand markets. And when I see a toy store, I always have a look around inside to see what's new.

Luckily, I have a great girlfriend who loves and collects toys, too, so we can stuff our house with all that plastic and vinyl. We even may have to move soon because we're running out of space.

---

1. Prescore all fold lines by gently running a craft knife down a straight edge.

2. Cut out all objects. Be sure to cut white lines between feet and face.

3. Fold feet front to back and glue.

4. Build the rest of BODY.

5. Glue ARMS on BODY matching letters.

6. Fold and glue BACKPACK together and glue on back of BODY where marked.

7. Glue PIZZA BOX LID together and place on top of BODY.

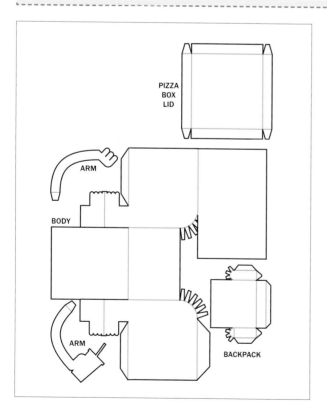

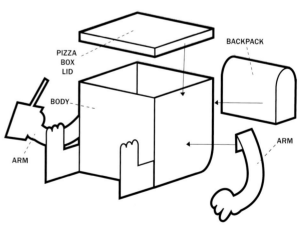

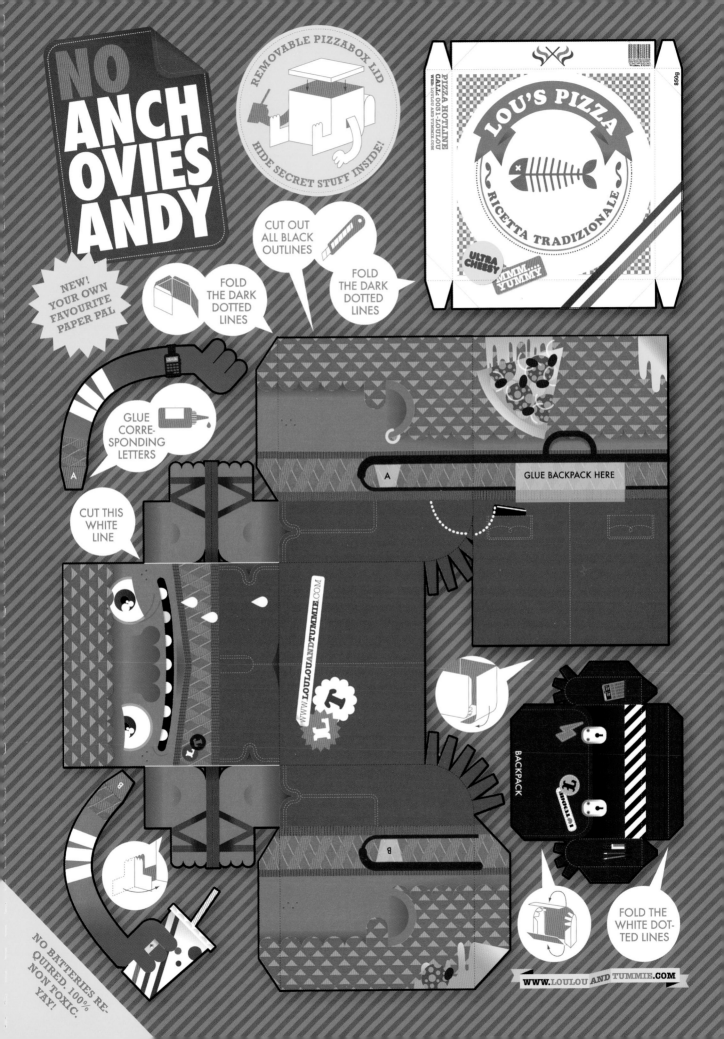

No. 2 **UNIT.2**

by Bryan Rollins
Jackson, Tennessee, USA

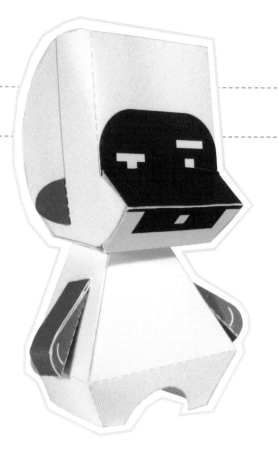

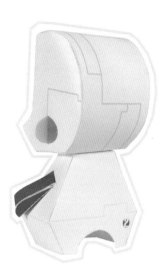

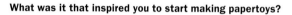

What was it that inspired you to start making papertoys?

Traditional origami, actually. In third grade, our teacher, Mrs. Carter, showed us how to make origami pinwheels. One of my classmates tweaked it and showed it to me—"Look, I made a robot"—and I thought it was so cool. (In retrospect, it looked more like a house with two pointy feet.) So, for the next eight years, I studied origami: books, sites, whatever. Joseph Wu became my best friend, and www.origami.com was my bible. Back then, my philosophy was: If you can't fold it from one square piece of paper without cutting it, it's not origami. Crazy, I know, but I think it was because of the impracticality. You can't sit in English class cutting paper.

After eleventh grade, I slacked up on the paper side of things and focused on college. In my sophomore year at Memphis College of Art, I got into the whole graffiti/street/lowbrow art culture and fashion, and stumbled upon an article on Hypebeast (www.hypebeast.com) about Shin Tanaka. Before that time, I was used to paper sculpture being toys, or model houses, or trains, or abstract isometrics. I was intrigued at how contemporary he'd made the medium, so I did a couple of his simpler models, and a few months later, I decided to do a custom Mask Hoody and send it to him. He liked it and put it in the series. After that, I was hooked. I discovered a whole paper craft underground world by way of blogs like Paper Forest and PaperKraft. net (http://paperkraft.blogspot.com), and I started to seek out interesting and complex paper models. After I got comfy, I did another custom of a Spiky Baby, and it ended up in the series as well. That was when I decided to start doing my own originals.

Can you tell us a little about your experience designing your first papertoy? How long did it take? What inspired the shape? What was the process you used to design it?

Well, my first three papertoys—Angel, Morilla and The Twins— were created to be sold at an art sale we were having at school. But really, I just wanted an excuse to motivate me to finally sit down and make a toy. As far as work hours, I'd say I put in about three whole days of work over a week, from sketches to the three finished constructed products. The designing process only took me about five hours before I got a polished template to design on top of, and two hours to have Angel's design complete and ready for print. I think that was because of my excitement.

The process I used back then isn't much different than what I'm using now. Angel was my first one, and she had been in my mind for a while, so all I really did was one quick sketch before I got started. I wanted the shape to be simple because I didn't want the complexity of the toy to overpower the design I was going to put on top of it (plus, I didn't really know what I was doing). I started by cutting out shapes and taping them together, which I call "scrap fitting." The body would comprise 90 percent of the model, so I had to make it interesting. That's when I made the tummy, which broke up the shape a little and made the model more distinctive. I also decided to make the arms and wings movable to add some kineticism to an otherwise static model. I always liked interactivity in other models I'd seen and built.

After the initial scrap fitting, I broke the parts down to look like what would be on the finished template, scanned them in, traced them in Adobe Illustrator, printed it, cut it out, had a "test fit-ting," made notes, tweaked the template in Illustrator according to the notes, printed the revised template, test fit, and be merry. The final test-fit model was what I drew onto for the flat design. After I was satisfied with the drawing, I scanned the parts and traced them in Illustrator, tweaked 'em, colored 'em and all that good stuff, and got ready to print on good paper for the final. All that took seven hours. The rest of the time was me churning out three of each original papertoy, which was a lot back then. I only sold one (ha!), but it was really fun. I'd do it again.

Do you enjoy working on other artists' templates?

Of course! Not only is it a learning experience, I get to have a free piece of artwork. I don't have the money for vinyl, so it's nice to have artists of the same caliber working in a medium accessible to anyone anywhere in the world. It's also pretty nice to turn on some music and spend some quiet time putting a few together. It's cool to see people's reactions when they see a shelf full of cute paper sculptures, like "I didn't even know paper could do that!"

I haven't had as much time for it since I started doing my own, but I still download them when I get a chance so I can build them in my downtime (read: when the Internet connection starts acting a fool).

What are some of the things that inspire your work?

I'm really inspired by cleverness. I really like music, movies, art and anything that achieves its purpose in a creative and unexpected way.

What do you think is the biggest advantage of working in paper? What's the biggest disadvantage?

Well, I guest the biggest advantage would be the accessibility and relative cheapness to produce a toy and have others be able to pick one up. I really can't see a disadvantage, per se, other than it being a tricky medium to work with, but what doesn't kill you…

---

1. Prescore all dotted fold lines by gently running a craft knife down a straight edge.

2. Cut out all objects. Be sure to cut arm slots on BODY.

3. Fold and glue BODY together.

4. Build ARMS and insert in slots on the side of BODY.

5. Glue middle of HEAD around the sides of HEAD.

6. Glue HEAD on top of BODY.

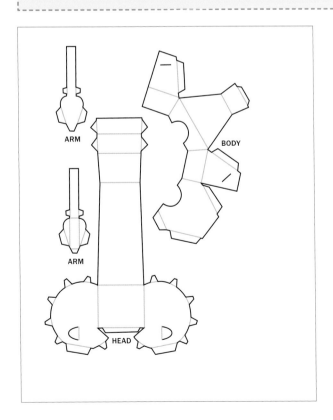

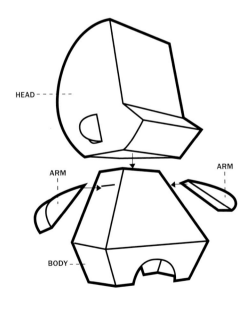

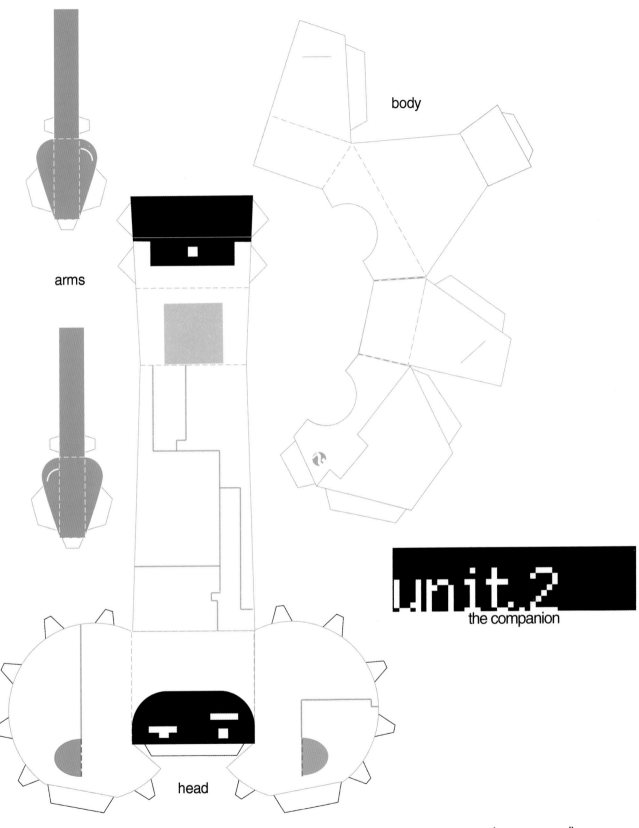

arms

body

head

unit.2
the companion

bryan rollins
youdontseeus.blogspot.com

No. 3 E440

by Ringo Krumbiegel
Amsterdam, The Netherlands

What inspired you to create the e440 project?

About two years ago, I saw a blank Dunny at a local toy store. Shortly after, I came across the Qee figurines and their many incarnations. Because there are simply too many vinyl toys available, and because they tend to be rather expensive, I decided to create a toy of my own, including a blank version for circulation. In this manner, everybody, including me, could get their hands on free designer toys.

Why a squirrel?

Initially, the toy resembled a cat rather than a squirrel. Then I read an article about the destruction of 440 squirrels at the Schiphol airport. In 1999, KLM Cargo cut 440 living squirrels into bits using a shredder because the required bills of health were missing. This inspired me to design a squirrel to be let loose on the Internet and thus regain its freedom. The aim of this project is to get 440 different interpretations of e440.

What does "e440" mean?

Simple. The "e" is derived from "eekhoorn" ["squirrel" in Dutch], and 440 is the number of slaughtered squirrels.

What was your process for coming up with the form?

I had a selection of small square medicine packages that I was stacking, turning and twisting, and so the first version consisted of nothing but squares and cubes. I dissected some of the pack-

ages and came up with my own forms. I also tried some more complex forms, but they turned out to be too difficult to build, and I really wanted to create something that anybody could make and customize.

You've had a lot of cool custom designs of e440 by other artists. Did you have in mind this would be a platform toy from the beginning?

Yes, I do want to reach 440 different designs, and I can certainly not reach that number by myself.

How did you get the word out about e440?

I first started the e440 blog. After issuing the blank template, I was asked for a small interview, which appeared on Toysrevil (www.toysrevil.net). Then you introduced the toy on Paper Forest (http://paperforest.blogspot.com), and e440 took off. You can also find e440 stickers all around the streets. These stickers are available for download from the e440 blog.

Do you have a favorite e440?

Many of the designs are very cool, yet one has a special place in my heart because it was the first custom I received. This was #11, the magnificent steam-powered squirrel by Lord Auron. It really is a magnificent design. I was very thrilled to find that someone actually had worked with my design. By the way, #11 has also become the most requested version of e440.

Can you tell us a little about the graphic design class who made use of your e440 template?

In the fall of 2007, I was asked by a lecturer of the Bangkok University International College whether he could use some of e440's designs for his graphic design classes. I told him he could, but thought little of it. After a while, I visited the university's site and to my surprise found out that creating an e440 skin had become part of the student curriculum. He promised he would send me the templates after he had graded them, but he hasn't answered any of my mail since.

What's in the future for e440? Any cool projects coming up?

I am toying with the idea of showing e440 in some sort of exhibition. Also, I am working on an enlarged version. It would be really cool to have an event at which the gigantic version will be spray painted by graffiti artists.

Would you like to see e440 as a vinyl toy someday?

That must be every papertoy creator's dream.

What has been the coolest thing that happened to you as a result of the e440 project?

There have been so many cool things. A review at toysrevil.net, a meeting with Amsterdam graffiti crew Kwasten Met De Gasten ["painting with the dudes"], an e440 design by DHM, who is a great graphic designer and street artist from Amsterdam, and, of course, being published in a book on papertoys. Cool, huh?

When you are not working on the e440 project, what do you do?

I am a supervisor of activities at a daycare center for demented elderly, so I am an amateur at graphic design. In my spare time, I paint, draw and build papertoys. I live a happy life together with my beloved wife and our soon-to-be firstborn.

What are some of the things that inspire you?

Anything can inspire me, as long as it has body, color and shape!

What advice would you give to someone who wanted to start his own papertoy project?

To examine the shapes of other papertoys and packages well. Ask yourself whether the shapes you choose can actually be built and customized. The more complex the shape is, the more complex the customizing will be. Learn of the work of others, but never copy. And then present your design at nicepapertoys.com, a wonderful meeting place for papertoy fans.

There seem to be quite a few papertoy designers from the Netherlands. Why do you think that is?

Dutch design is appreciated worldwide, and has been for quite some time. Think of Rietveld, Harvink, Berlage, Escher, Marcel Wanders and many others. We also boast one of the world's leading design academies, based in Eindhoven. Good design is omnipresent, and everybody grows up with it.

---

1. Prescore all dotted fold lines by gently running a craft knife down a straight edge.

2. Cut out all objects.

3. Fold and glue ears front to back build HEAD.

4. Glue tab with "g*" on belly first then add two coins for weight on inside of belly panel. Finish building BODY.

5. Fold and glue RIGHT and LEFT LEGS.

6. Fold and glue ARMS and TAIL.

7. Glue all parts on BODY by matching up yellow areas.

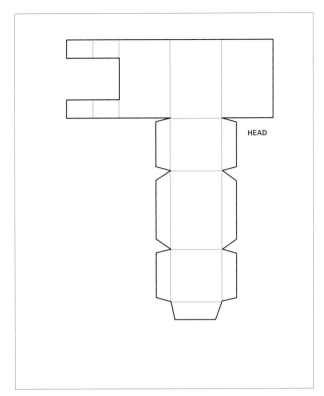

HEAD

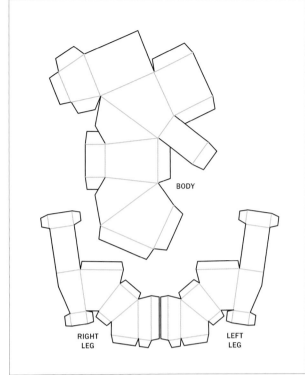

BODY

RIGHT
LEG

LEFT
LEG

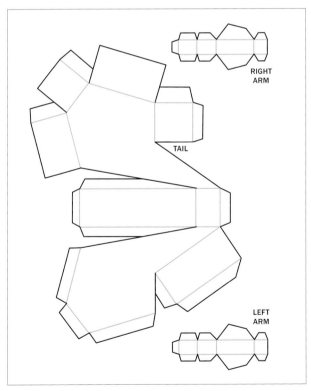

RIGHT
ARM

TAIL

LEFT
ARM

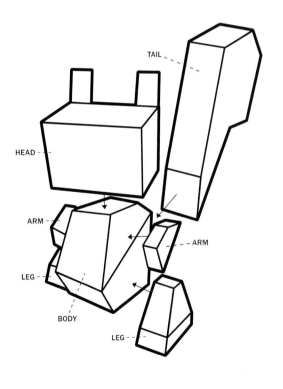

TAIL

HEAD

ARM

ARM

LEG

BODY

LEG

#02 Camouflage

Use thick, sturdy paper [I use 235 grams matt-coated photo paper].
First cut along the outlines with a sharp knife.
Dotted lines are folding lines; incise. Do not cut through the paper.
First fold all parts and then glue.
Areas marked with 'g' are mating surfaces.
Assemble all parts separately before constructing the model.
Cut away excess paper if necessary.
Yellow areas mark the locations where the squirrel's parts connect.
First connect the tail to the body, then the head to the body, then the hind legs and forelegs.
Read, look and think before you cut and use glue!
Feed me back your suggestions, questions etc.
Have fun!

g

g

g

g

g

g

g

body

Fold the top of the ears to the back to cover the back

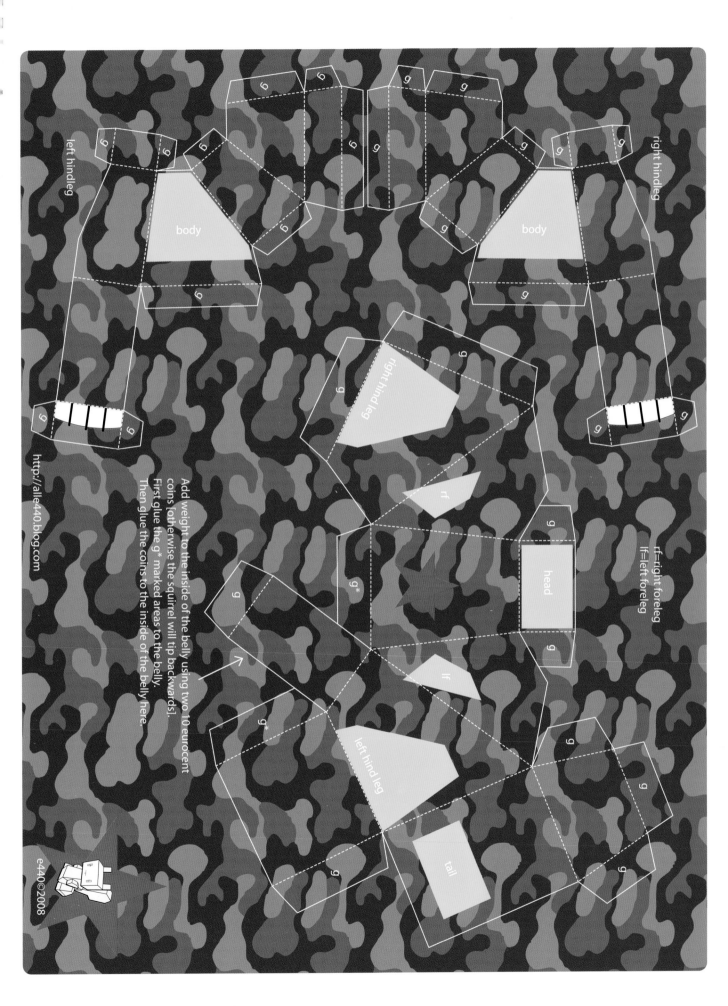

left hindleg

right hindleg

body

body

right hind leg

rf

g*

head

g*

lf

left hind leg

tail

rf=right foreleg
lf=left foreleg

Add weight to the inside of the belly using two 10 eurocent coins (otherwise the squirrel will tip backwards).
First glue the g* marked areas to the belly.
Then glue the coins to the inside of the belly here.

http://alle440.blog.com

e440©2008

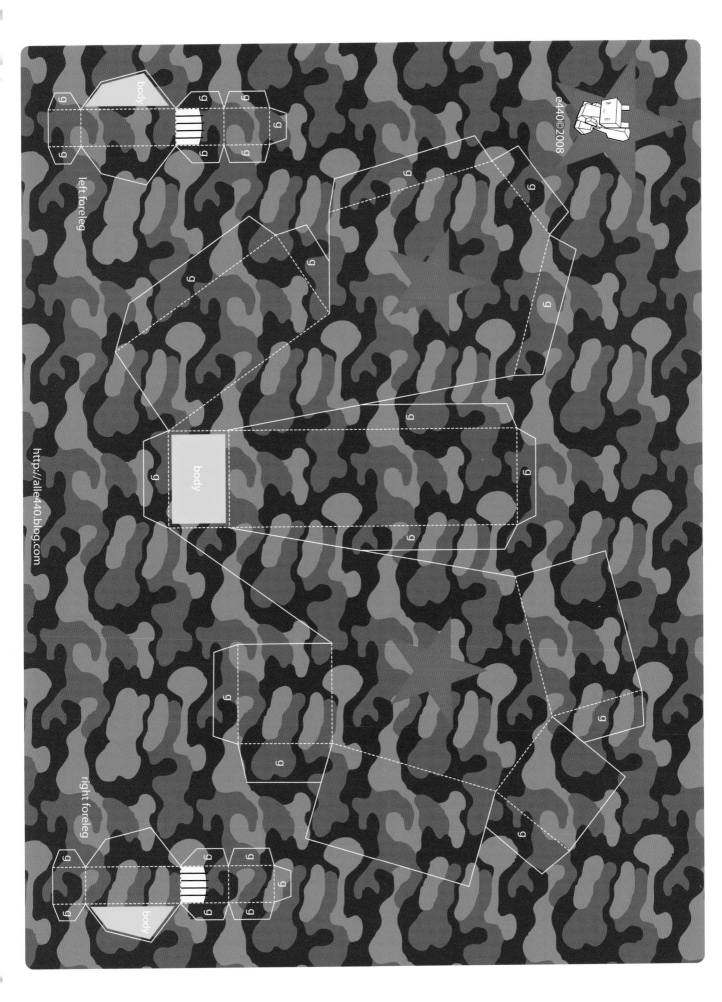

left foreleg

body

body

right foreleg

body

No. 4 **SIZZA**

by Nick Knite
Essen, Germany

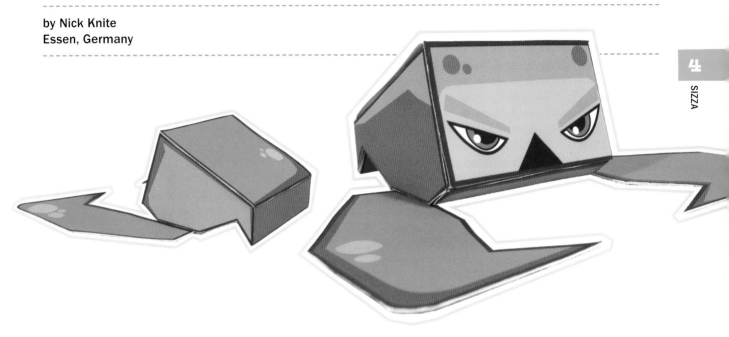

Who or what is a SIZZA?

SIZZA is a just recently discovered sub-species of the crab family. The original one was found at a rocky beach somewhere on the coast of Germany. As the research for his origin continued, there were other members of the SIZZA family discovered, not only in Germany but also in France, Italy, Spain and even across the ocean in the United States and South America. Probably there are even more, but they are yet to be discovered.

Why did you decide to document SIZZA as a papertoy?

Paper seemed so obvious and practical! I wanted the sketch and illustration to come to life, and plush and vinyl weren't "available," for I am no good at knitting and 3-D CAD [computer-aided design]. I found other designers like Readymech, Marshall Alexander and Shin Tanaka on the Internet and thought, "That's it." The easy way of getting SIZZA out there! It took some time to get it right, loads of early SIZZA paper versions are still sitting on my shelf, but the minute I put together the first printout, I knew that this would become what I wanted for SIZZA.

Are vinyl and plush still something you would like to explore for SIZZA in the future?

Definitely—both, actually. Although I have to rely on the help of others there. That's why paper was the first, fastest and, for me, best choice to get him out there. I was able to do the designing and "sculpting" myself, no sewing or 3-D programming skills necessary. Plus, paper makes customizing, in order

to explore all the different styles of SIZZA, way easier than any other material.

You've got a lot of cool custom SIZZAs by other artists on your blog. Was that something you had in mind when you first launched SIZZA, for it to be kind of a paper platform toy?

Actually, yes! I always loved the idea of a platform toy, just like Kidrobot's Munny and Dunny. To see what other people come up with, how much further they take the design, to see all the things made that I didn't think of. So far, it has worked out perfectly! I couldn't tell you which custom is my favorite, because they all are fantastic in their own way. Each artist took a different approach toward SIZZA, and I love that. That was exactly what I intended! So, a simple "yes" would have probably been enough to answer your question.

Can you tell us a little about Funk Food?

Funk Food is my creative output. The name actually came from mix tapes I used to make. I came up with a couple of logos and designs for it, and it kind of became my brand. Right now, I am using the name for all my creative activities. I plan to hopefully produce the SIZZA as a vinyl toy someday but probably in the rounder shape as in my logo for SIZZA. I am also working on a clothing line and as a graphic-design firm.

With all that stuff going, how do you stay inspired?

Good question! I don't really know, besides surfing the Internet and keeping my eyes open everywhere I go. There is so much inspiration all around me, it is sometimes just hard to get it "translated" into another medium, such as drawing or even on the computer. Plus, I sometimes don't really even think of myself as that creative when I see guys like you, the other artists you feature and those who put their stuff out there on the web. But then again, I am in here, too, right? So I must've done something right.

If SIZZA had to get a day job, what do you think it would be?

Hm. I think he would be a lifeguard on the beach! Red trunks on, a rescue buoy at his side and beautiful ladies all around, just like in *Baywatch*!

---

1. Prescore all fold lines by gently running a craft knife down a straight edge.

2. Cut out all objects. Be sure to cut up lines between CLAWS and BODY as shown in diagram on toy.

3. Fold and glue CLAWS front to back.

4. For the BODY, glue bottom to sides.

5. Glue top of BODY to side and glue FACE last.

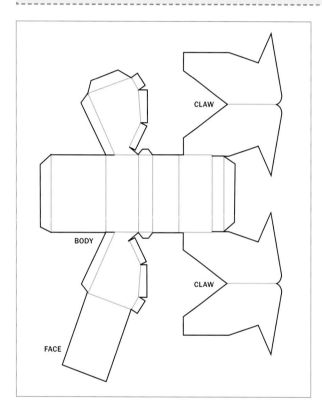

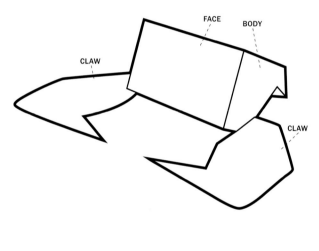

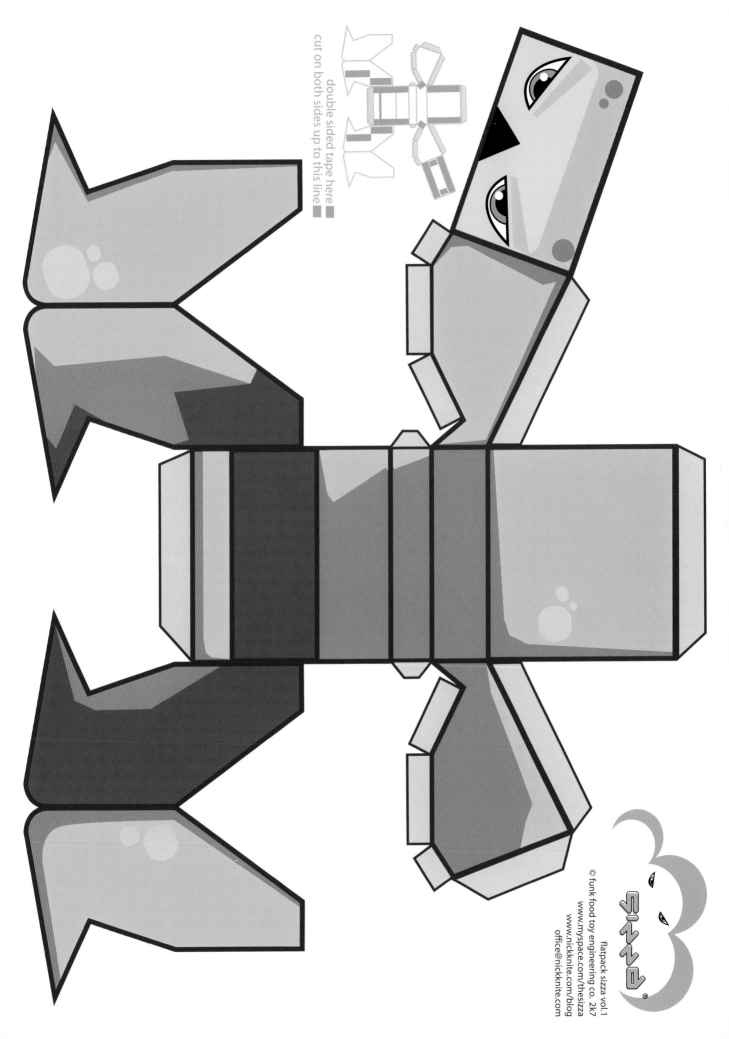

double sided tape here
cut on both sides up to this line

flatpack sizza vol.1
© funk food toy engineering co. 2k7
www.myspace.com/thesizza
www.nickknite.com/blog
office@nickknite.com

No. 5 **MAX 95**

by Jon Greenwell, a.k.a. Jonny Chiba
Liverpool, England

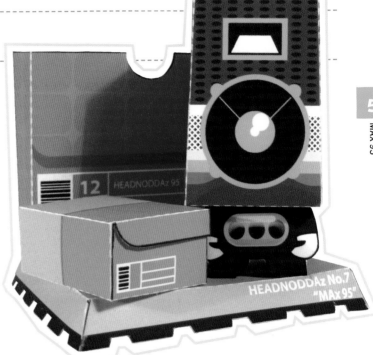

What inspired you to start cranking out papertoys, and what was your first?

I guess the first thing that inspired me, or showed me the possibilities, could have been a "font pack" by House Industries. As part of the promotion for a family of fonts, they produced a card model [paper craft] custom van. After this, I made a few card models of trucks, buses, trains, etc., purely to put graffiti on them. As for character work, I've been interested in vinyl models for a while, and when the "play beast-card boy" (part vinyl, part card) model dropped, I decided to make something similar. The end result being the Pixel Ninja—a simple square head and box-like body. I deliberately tried to make the body look different from the card boy models, as the square head was pretty similar.

Your HEADNODDAz blog has a lot of fun customs, from the Cheech Wizard to the four elements of hip-hop (Graffiti, Emcee, Deejay and Bboy) of your HEADNODDAz toy, a cool little dude with an amp for a head. They all have their own little set pieces, too. What was your inspiration for this series?

I've been into vinyl toys for a while, but a lack of money means I was never a serious collector, so I hit upon the idea of making my own. My idea for the HEADNODDAz was to create a one-sheet model that was simple to make. So after coming up with the original form, it was just a question of simplifying it, yet keeping the "character" of it. I wanted a backdrop behind them, to make them stand on their own, in their own identifiable space. Plus, it gives more space to illustrate on, and adds depth to

the model. As for inspiration, I guess it all flows back to a love of hip-hop, all four elements of it. That's where the boombox comes from. I'm still trawling secondhand stores looking for the perfect iconic one. Once I'd discarded the boombox as head and moved it to a background piece, it was a question of coming up with something for a head that would fit the proportions of the model. I'd seen Tim Sui's vinyl speakers, so opted for an amp head, so I can't say it's original. The name HEADNODDAz came from an old Brooklyn Funk Essentials track, "A Headnaddas Journey to the Planet Adidi-Skizm."

Any tips for people who want to design their own papertoys?

1. Keep it simple. The simpler it is, the more chance there is people will make it.

2. Keep the number of sheets of paper used as low as possible. A fifteen-sheet model will be daunting to some people.

3. Don't be afraid to keep refining a model until you're happy with it. If it looks good as a blank, white model, think what it will look like "textured."

4. If you have access to 3-D modeling tools, use them, but don't get carried away with polygons. Remember, you've got to make this.

5. Learn from the vinyl toy scene. A blank, customizable model gives people the chance to stamp their own identities on your model.

6. Make sure you have plenty of shelf space.

Papertoys do seem to multiply awfully fast. When you're not busy making great papertoys for folks to download, what are you up to?

By day, I'm a senior artist in a games development company, mainly creating environments, although I do some background character work. I've been doing it since the days of PlayStation one, so I'm fairly well versed in 3-D modeling. I have a daughter, so I tend not to have too much spare time, but what little I have, I fill with design, graffiti and music. I have loads of ideas floating around my head and in sketchbooks for characters, T-shirts, mixtapes. It's just a question of finding the time to do justice to them all. I keep thinking I'll do some T-shirt designs, and put them on my blog and let people print them out themselves if they like them. I'm working on a PDF portfolio that I can make available on my blog. It's just a question of editing it down. I also tend to take hour-long baths and read.

What does your daughter think of your papertoys?

My daughter likes the toys, but I think she prefers the cuter, more Japanese-style ones than the HEADNODDAz. I've tried giving her a design sheet to color, but I think she prefers ownership of her own projects (clay models, etc.). Maybe I will make one of her designs into a HEADNODDA.

Have you ever thought about trying to sell your papertoys?

I've never really thought about selling any models. I like the fact that things on the Internet are free, and that you are allowed to reach a wider audience than immediate friends. I think if anyone was interested in using my models, and I liked the project, I would allow them to be used free of charge. I have a creative day job, so the paper models are more like a hobby. I like treating them as a design challenge, trying to come up with new forms. I guess if I were doing them to order, they would become less enjoyable.

---

1. Prescore all dotted fold lines by gently running a craft knife down a straight edge.

2. Cut out all objects.

3. Fold and glue the BASE and BACKDROP together.

4. Glue BACKDROP to the back of BASE.

5. Fold and glue HEAD and BODY together.

6. Glue HEAD to the top of BODY.

7. Fold and glue SHOEBOX together.

8. Place figure and SHOEBOX on BASE.

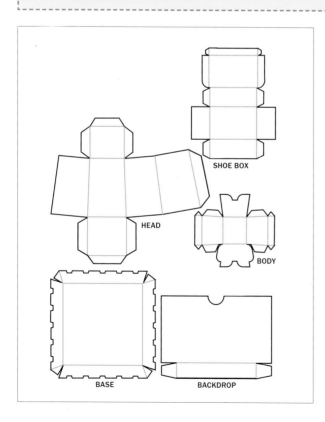

SHOE BOX

HEAD

BODY

BASE

BACKDROP

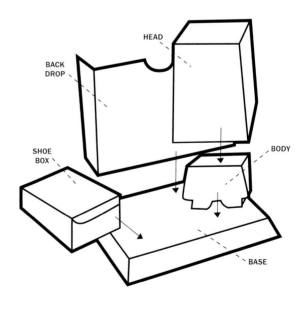

HEAD

BACK DROP

SHOE BOX

BODY

BASE

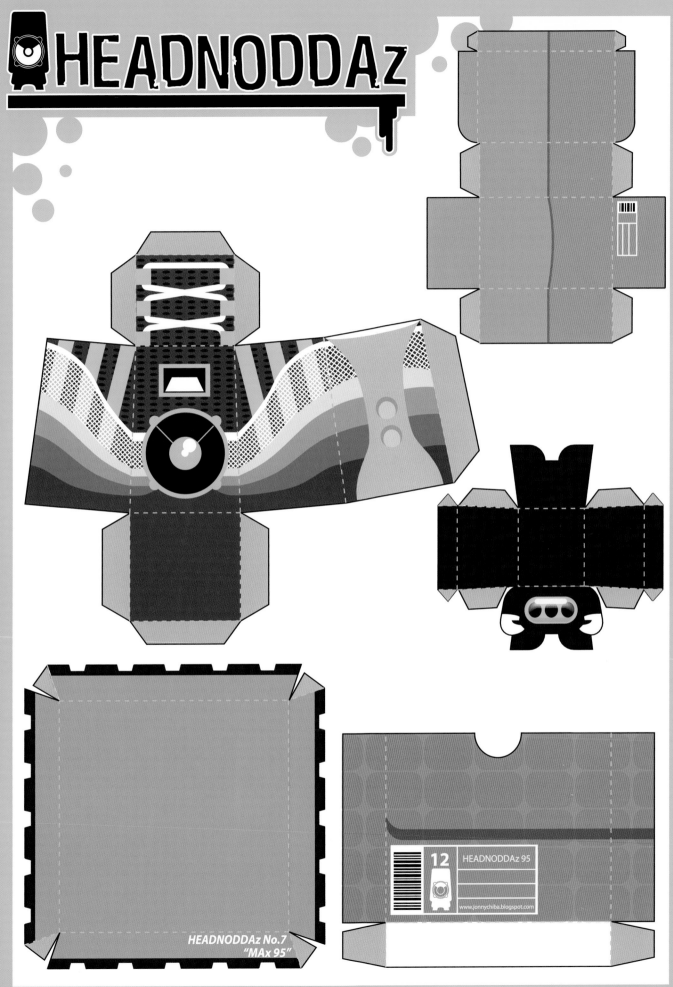

HEADNODDAz

HEADNODDAz 95

12

HEADNODDAz No.7
"MAx 95"

No. 6 **BOXY**

by Shin Tanaka
Fukuoka, Japan

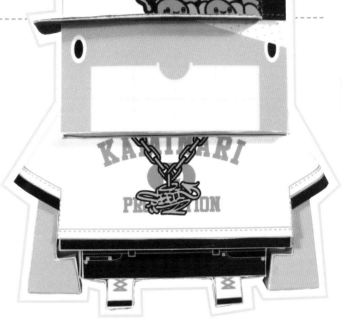

What inspired you to start making papertoys?

It's a jealousy of vinyl toys.

What do you think is the biggest advantage of working in paper?

Many people can enjoy it easily. Easy to make, easy to customize.

What's the biggest disadvantage?

The quality of the toy depends on the hand skills of who builds it up. It's also weak in water.

Can you tell us a little bit about your process for designing a new papertoy?

I don't use any 3-D modeling software; I don't like polygonal and box shapes. Therefore, I repeat drawing lines, cutting it out, building it up and modifying the lines many times. It makes my papertoys have rounded and smooth shapes.

A lot of great designers have done customs on your papertoy templates. How did these collaborations with other artists start?

In my case, I haven't called for design; my works became popular by word of mouth. When I collaborate with an artist, his friends check it out and ask me if they can make one of their own too.

You have a lot of great papertoys—Boxy, T-Boy, Gritty, Spiky. Is there one that is your favorite?

T-Boy is my favorite one; it's my representative model. And it has an element of street fashion.

What inspires you?

Hip-hop culture inspires me. I love hip-hop music, and I was always listening to hip-hop music when I made a design or built a toy up.

What do you think about the recent proliferation of designer papertoys on the 'net?

It has a good influence and a bad influence. It increased a chance that people know about papertoys, but most of recent papertoys are not high quality, I think. We are trying to raise the level up to art. But not high-quality projects are disturbing our efforts.

Your work has been featured on several vinyl toys. Are there any plans to do any of your papertoys in vinyl?

Yes, I have a few plans to make my characters in vinyl. To my great delight, many people say they love my toys. They not only love my style that I make something from paper, but they also simply love my character design. I'd like to delivery my toys to them, but my papertoys are only for display. Therefore, many companies are helping me to make them in vinyl and deliver them to my fans.

What has been the coolest thing that has happened to you because of your papertoy work?

I make many friends via my papertoys. I have gotten to know more than 300 artists from all over the world! Papertoys are bringing me new friends every day.

What do you see in the future for papertoys?

It would be bipolar evaluations. Some pursue the quality, and others pursue simplicity. Because it's not difficult to start their own papertoy projects, however, it's difficult to keep the fascination. Maybe many more people start new papertoy projects, but most of them are dumped into the dustbin. Hopefully the designers will keep the quality higher so that papertoys can survive.

1. Prescore all fold lines by gently running a craft knife down a straight edge.

2. Cut out all objects. Be sure to cut red line above eyes for HAT BILL.

3. Fold and glue HAT BILL front to back. Insert into HEAD through red slot and glue tabs inside.

4. Fold and glue HEAD and PANTS.

5. Fold and glue ARMS.

6. Fold and glue SHIRT. Glue SLEEVE TRIM to the bottom insides of sleeves so the black part shows. Glue the longer piece of SHIRT TRIM to the bottom inside of the front and sides. Glue the short piece of SHIRT TRIM to the bottom inside of the back of SHIRT.

7. Put ARMS inside sleeves of SHIRT and glue tabs at the end of ARMS inside sleeves.

8. Glue HEAD inside SHIRT collar.

9. Insert PANTS inside SHIRT.

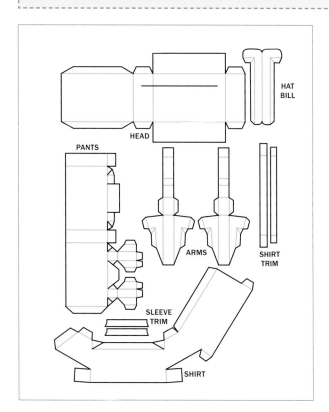

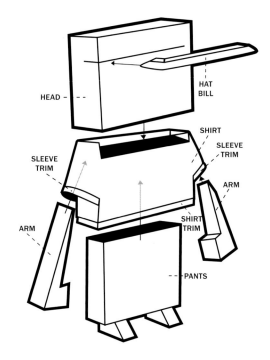

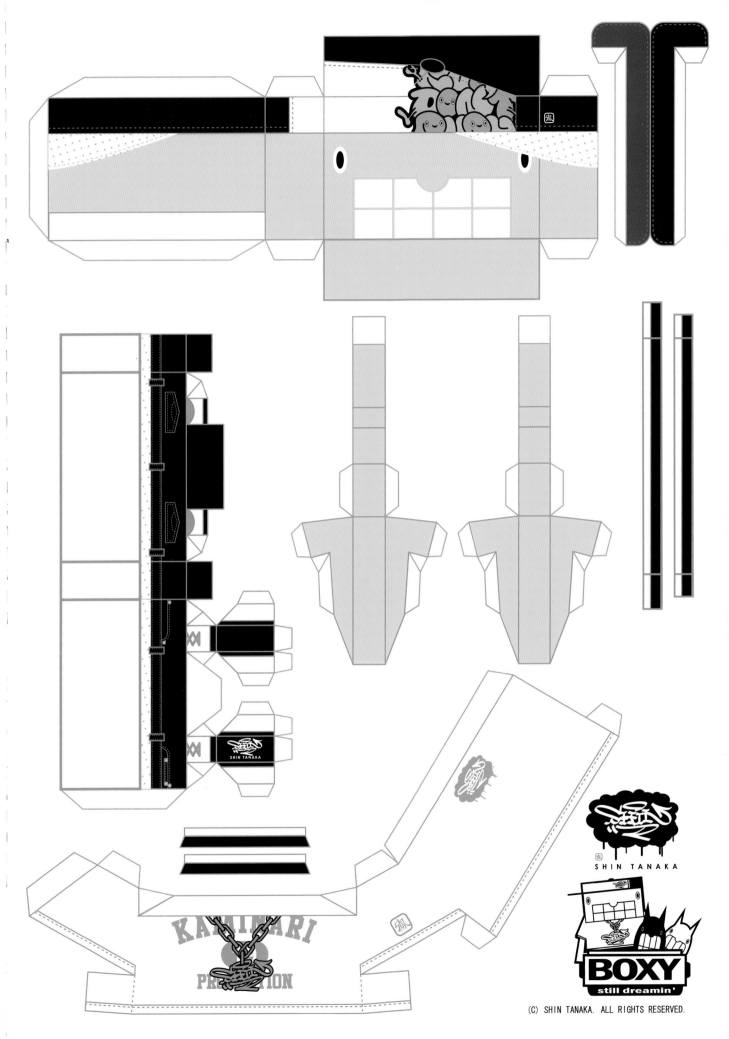

No. 7 **MICRO TOYPAPER**

by Rememberthelittleguy
Manchester, England

What inspired you to start Toypaper?

I guess like most designers I have always loved illustration, design, toys and the whole culture that fits in between. When I attended the second Pictoplasma conference in Berlin, I was exposed to so much inspiration in those four days that when I got back home, I just wanted to start making things. The first task I set myself was to make myself some new business cards that, when folded, stood up to form a little character. I showed a friend of mine my new creations, and he pointed me to some characters from Fwis and the amazing Shin [Tanaka]. Their work really pushed me to create my first model, then after a few more, they needed their own place to live—and Toypaper was born.

How was the reception for Toypaper starting out? Did you get a lot of downloads? What did you do to get the word out about Toypaper?

When I made my first Toypaper model, I put it on my site as a little hidden extra for reading some of my news. After a couple of weeks, I noticed that nearly 170 people had downloaded the PDF, so I put it as a main button on the home page, and nearly 300 people had downloaded it the next week. That made me design some more monsters and try those on the site, too. It was after a month that I really saw an opportunity for a brand new project, but the downside was that I had to upgrade to a bigger hosting package as I went over my limit one week and ended having to pay £15 for just two days' usage! I don't mind, though. It's worth it just to get a few e-mails every day from people around the world who you wouldn't necessarily ever meet

in your life. It also has really made me push my illustration and Flash work, too, which is never a bad thing. At the last count, my visitors for the last two years was just over 240,000, and nearly 2,000 people have signed up to the Toypaper mailing list.

The first really big thing that happened was a custom Toypaper session at Sketch City in Manchester, England. Sketch City is a collective that brings together a whole manner of talented folks to do live illustration and painting in a bar, drawing on huge canvases and tabletops to some really good live music. I created some blank, easy-to-make Toypaper templates for everyone to have a try, and Jon at Sketch City very kindly brought some scissors, Pritt Sticks [glue] and marker pens for everyone to do their thing with.

What inspires you?

I love meeting new people and seeing their work, especially when you are in a bit of a low patch and you find so much inspiration in their work that it makes you crack your sketchbook open and start scribbling. I work with some really great people, too, so during the day, there are so many links being e-mailed around that you discover a lot of things that you wouldn't necessarily find yourself.

What advice would you give people who want to design their own papertoys?

Start with a simple box, then add little things as you go on. Don't be scared to experiment. I have a drawer full of papertoys that never quite made it!

Oh, buy a good scalpel, metal ruler and cutting mat—they are your new tools of the trade.

How do you go about designing a new papertoy?

It always starts with a sketch, then I try to break the sketch down into sections that are possible to fold. More often than not, though, I tweak and redesign as I go along. Normally, I will design, print, build, amend, print, build, amend, etc., until I am happy with it, or until I completely lose patience.

When you're not busy with Toypaper.com, what do you do?

I am an interaction designer based in the UK, so I spend my daytime designing, concepting, animating—it's really nice.

What is the best thing about working with paper? What's the most challenging thing?

Learning things that you didn't want to learn at school! I found I was determining angles to make sure my folds were in the right place and making calculations about paper thickness in relation to the number of folds a piece has.

Because I love building the toys, it doesn't feel like learning. Maybe if they taught papertoy design in schools, math would become a happy place.

What's in the future for Toypaper.com? Any cool projects in the works?

I am releasing some limited-run retail toys this year, plus a super-size exhibition coming up with tiny two-centimeter Toypapers in the same room as fifteen-foot ones. I am also working with the nice chaps at Rebus Collective on a clothing collaboration. We are exploring a lot of different ways to interact with the items after you have bought them. It is all linked up via the web—very simple and hopefully addictive! I hope Toypaper continues to introduce me to some amazing people. I love the e-mails and photos that people send. I have a growing mailing list and some community projects lined up, which hopefully will bring members together from around the world and create new friendships—and all new Toypapers.

1. Prescore all dotted fold lines by gently running a craft knife down a straight edge.

2. Cut out all objects. Be sure to cut out the screen window.

3. Fold and glue ARMS together; see diagram on toy.

4. Glue BODY together, following diagram on toy.

5. Fold and glue slide-in SCREENS front to back and slide into front window of BODY.

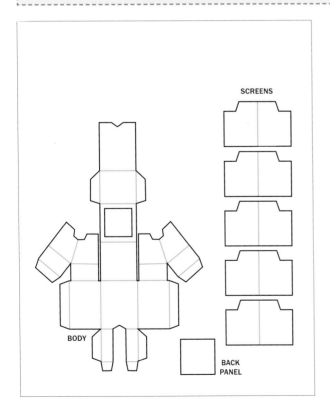

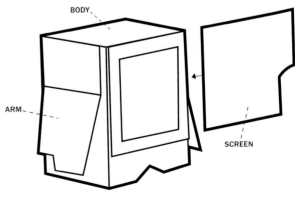

BE A SAFETY SOLDIER TAKE CARE OF THOSE LITTLE FINGERS

MICRO: MAIN BODY

MICRO² SLIDE-IN SCREENS

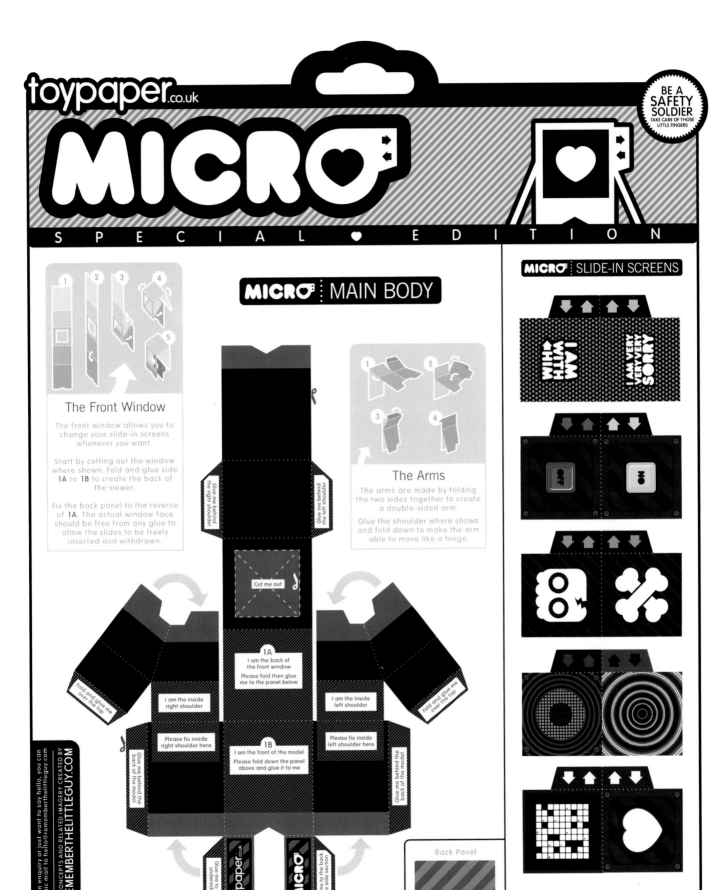

The Front Window

The front window allows you to change your slide-in screens whenever you want.

Start by cutting out the window where shown. Fold and glue side **1A** to **1B** to create the back of the viewer.

Fix the back panel to the reverse of **1A**. The actual window face should be free from any glue to allow the slides to be freely inserted and withdrawn.

The Arms

The arms are made by folding the two sides together to create a double-sided arm.

Glue the shoulder where shown and fold down to make the arm able to move like a hinge.

Glue me behind the right shoulder

Glue me behind the left shoulder

Cut me out

Fold and glue me over the top

Fold and glue me over the top

1A
I am the back of the front window.
Please fold then glue me to the panel below

I am the inside right shoulder

I am the inside left shoulder

Please fix inside right shoulder here

1B
I am the front of the model
Please fold down the panel above and glue it to me

Please fix inside left shoulder here

Glue me behind the back of the model

Glue me behind the back of the model

Glue me to the underside

Glue me to the back of the side section

toypaper.co.uk

MICRO²

Glue me

Glue me

Back Panel

I AM WITH HIM

I AM VERY VERY VERY SORRY

OFF

ON

Fold each one of these screens down the central fold line to create 5 double-sided interchangeable screenfaces for your Micro:Message

If you have an enquiry or just want to say hello, you can send electronic mail to hello@rememberthelittleguy.com

ALL DESIGN, CONCEPTS AND RELATED IMAGERY CREATED BY
WWW.REMEMBERTHELITTLEGUY.COM

IMPORTANT

FOLD · · · · · ·
CUT – – – –

GLUE

Read any special instructions before cutting. Please take care when using sharp items. Score dotted lines and cut dashed lines. Loosely assemble before applying glue.

MICRO:MESSAGE
DIFFICULTY: MEDIUM :: TIME: 20m

toypaper.co.uk
MICRO
S P E C I A L ● E D I T I O N

MICRO : MAIN BODY

The Front Window

The front window allows you to change your slide-in screens whenever you want.

Start by cutting out the window where shown. Fold and glue side **1A** to **1B** to create the back of the viewer.

Fix the back panel to the reverse of **1A**. The actual window face should be free from any glue to allow the slides to be freely inserted and withdrawn.

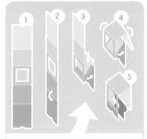

The Arms

The arms are made by folding the two sides together to create a double-sided arm.

Glue the shoulder where shown and fold down to make the arm able to move like a hinge.

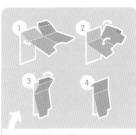

Glue me behind the right shoulder

Glue me behind the left shoulder

Cut me out

Fold and glue me over the top

Fold and glue me over the top

I am the inside right shoulder

I am the inside left shoulder

1A
I am the back of the front window.
Please fold then glue me to the panel below

Please fix inside right shoulder here

Please fix inside left shoulder here

1B
I am the front of the model
Please fold down the panel above and glue it to me

Glue me behind the back of the model

Glue me behind the back of the model

Glue me to the underside

toypaper.co.uk

MICRO

Glue me to the back of the side section

Glue me

Glue me

Back Panel

MICRO : SLIDE-IN SCREENS

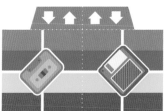

Fold each one of these screens down the central fold line to create 5 double-sided interchangeable screenfaces for your Micro:Message

If you have an enquiry or just want to say hello, you can send electronic mail to hello@rememberthelittleguy.com

ALL DESIGN, CONCEPTS AND RELATED IMAGERY CREATED BY
WWW.REMEMBERTHELITTLEGUY.COM

IMPORTANT

FOLD · · · · ·
CUT - - - -

GLUE Glue me

Read any special instructions before cutting. Please take care when using sharp items. Score dotted lines and cut dashed lines. Loosely assemble before applying glue.

MICRO:MESSAGE
DIFFICULTY: MEDIUM :: TIME: 20m

toypaper.co.uk

MICRO

SPECIAL ● EDITION

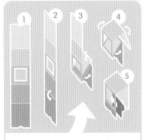

The Front Window

The front window allows you to change your slide-in screens whenever you want.

Start by cutting out the window where shown. Fold and glue side **1A** to **1B** to create the back of the viewer.

Fix the back panel to the reverse of **1A**. The actual window face should be free from any glue to allow the slides to be freely inserted and withdrawn.

MICRO : MAIN BODY

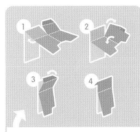

The Arms

The arms are made by folding the two sides together to create a double-sided arm.

Glue the shoulder where shown and fold down to make the arm able to move like a hinge.

Glue me behind the right shoulder

Glue me behind the left shoulder

Cut me out

fold and glue me over the top

Fold and glue me over the top

1A
I am the back of the front window.
Please fold then glue me to the panel below

I am the inside right shoulder

I am the inside left shoulder

Please fix inside right shoulder here

Please fix inside left shoulder here

1B
I am the front of the model
Please fold down the panel above and glue it to me

Glue me behind the back of the model

Glue me behind the back of the model

Glue me to the underside

toypaper.co.uk

MICRO

Glue me to the back of the side section

Glue me

Glue me

Back Panel

MICRO : SLIDE-IN SCREENS

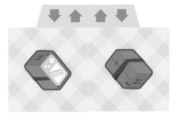

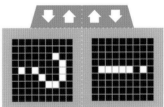

Fold each one of these screens down the central fold line to create 5 double-sided interchangeable screenfaces for your Micro:Message

---

IMPORTANT

FOLD · · · · ·
CUT ▪ ▪ ▪ ▪ ▪

GLUE | Glue me

Read any special instructions before cutting. Please take care when using sharp items. Score dotted lines and cut dashed lines. Loosely assemble before applying glue.

MICRO:MESSAGE
DIFFICULTY: MEDIUM :: TIME: 20m

No. 8 **BIGCHIEF TOY**

by BigChief Design
Milan, Italy

Can you tell us a little bit about BigChief Design? Give us a little history and what you do.

BigChief Design is a Milan-based digital communication and graphic design company founded by young, passionate and inspired people with diverse backgrounds and expertise, from marketing to design and visual communication to technology. We work in graphic design and illustrations, digital and interactive media.

What inspired the BigChief paper toy?

BigChief has been inspired from our love for design and art toys, and at the same time, we wanted to create something freely downloadable to thank our readers, and here he comes! It represents our way of giving something back to all the readers of our blog [http://think.bigchief.it] who have gotten us this far. BigChief Toy is an iconic graphic character, a twelve-centimeter-tall 3-D paper character. BigChief is a mustached man with a childish soul. He often says profound things. BigChief is also moody and absent-minded, but he's a good man with people who deserve it!

Was his look based on someone, or was he totally made up?

He is totally made up. The designer is Luca Gentile, and he got inspiration from the skater and street style world. He wanted to give to BigChief a touch of a "hard man" (a truck driver) also, so here it is—the detail of the mustache!

Does anybody at BigChief Design rock a big mustache like the BigChief paper toy?

No, but now anyone can have his own paper mustache, downloadable from http://think.bigchief.it.

This little guy has been popping up everywhere. How did you go about getting the word out about your papertoy?

The viral effect was created by word of mouth through sites, blogs and social networks, and it paid off in a very short timescale. To date, the toy has been downloaded by 9,000 users and received positive reviews on over fifty blogs and sites and reviews in magazines like *Glamour* and *Computer Arts Projects*. Then came the collaboration with other designers, like Mike Giles of the Canadian product design company Furni Creations, which led to the creation of a limited-edition personalized toy bearing the company's logo. The increased visibility of this project has opened up new communication channels. The idea of BigChief's "disappearance" was launched in order to boost the viral effect and to create a strong sense of community around the character of BigChief. Readers from all around the world were asked to send in photos and information of his sightings. These continue to arrive and are published online on Flickr, a photo-sharing social network.

Sounds like this little papertoy has opened some big doors for you! What's next for BigChief?

We're creating new collaborations, connections and contaminations, both with artists and companies. We are always looking for new ideas, inspiration and stimuli. We are always ready to have new experiences and meet people. We have been experimenting with cultural and media contamination. We love challenging ourselves and our partners to think outside the box.

Any words of wisdom from BigChief himself?

Have fun!

1. Prescore all fold lines by gently running a craft knife down a straight edge.

2. Cut out all objects.

3. Fold and glue BODY.

4. Cut the line between HANDS and BODY. Fold HANDS away from BODY.

5. Fold and glue HEAD.

6. Fold and glue HAT, and glue to HEAD. Bend HAT BILL up.

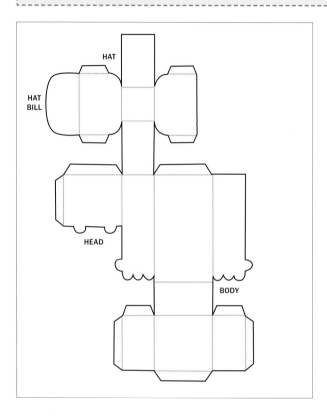

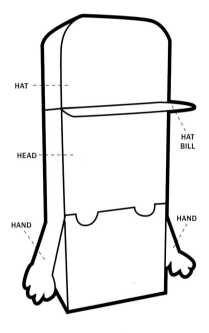

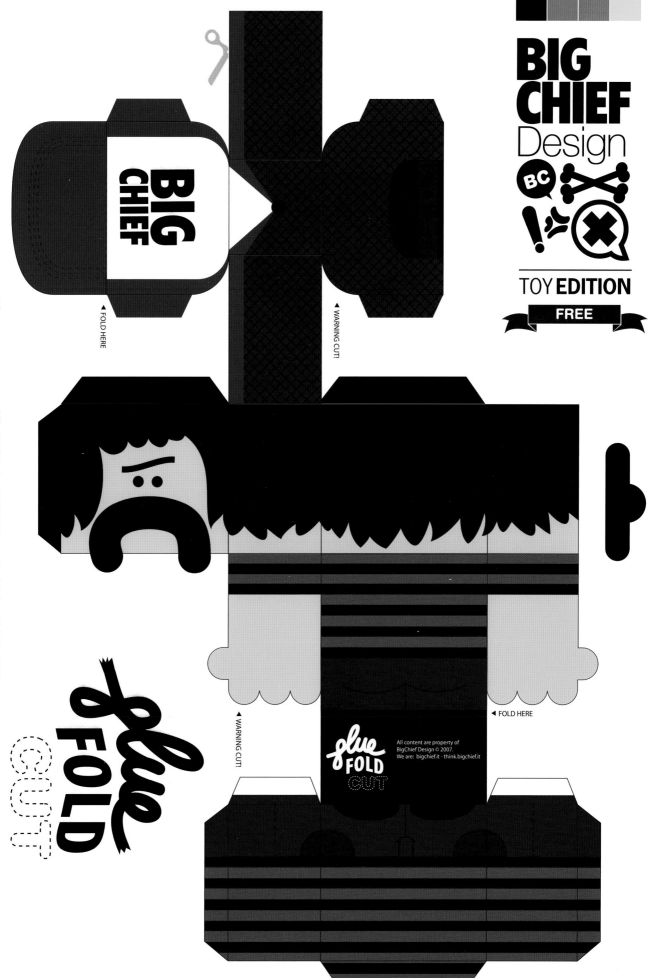

BIG CHIEF

▲ FOLD HERE

◄ WARNING CUT!

■■■■■

BIG CHIEF Design

BC

TOY EDITION

FREE

All content are propery of BigChief Design © 2007. We are: bigchief.it - think.bigchief.it

◄ WARNING CUT!

◄ FOLD HERE

glue FOLD CUT

All content are property of BigChief Design © 2007. We are: bigchief.it - think.bigchief.it

glue FOLD CUT

No. 9 **BURLABOX**

by Atelier Alessio Blanco
Viareggio, Lucca, Italy

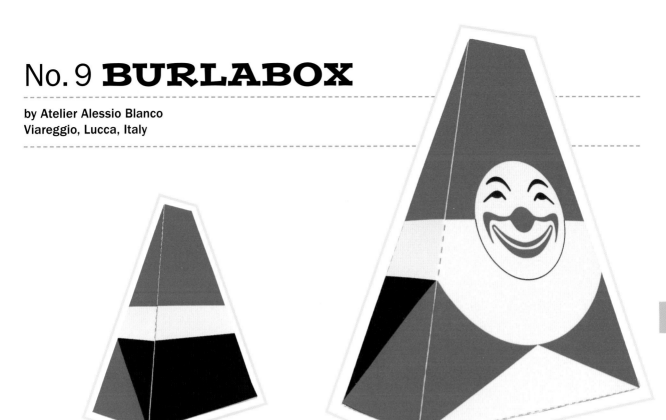

What is Atelier Alessio Blanco?

Atelier Alessio Blanco is a collective identity composed by various artists, architects and designers. We operate throughout Italy, mainly in Milan (Lombardy) and Viareggio (Tuscany), where we live.

Can you give us a little introduction to Burlamacco, Viareggio and its carnival?

Viareggio is a city located in Tuscany on the coast of the Tyrrhenian Sea, and it's the main center of the northern Tuscan Riviera known as Versilia.

Viareggio is known as a seaside resort, as well as being the home of the famous carnival of Viareggio, unanimously considered the most important carnival celebration of Italy and Europe. This famous carnival, dating back to 1873, is characterized by its papier-mâché floats parade along the promenade in the weeks preceding Easter. Burlamacco is the official mask that presides over the carnival and is the town's mascot. Burlamacco was drawn for the first time in 1930 by Uberto Bonetti.

Seventy-seven years later, Burlabox was born.

What was your inspiration to make a paper version of Burlamacco?

Before being a papertoy or an object design, Burlabox was a tribute to the city of Viareggio and its people, who love Burlamacco as their icon. We love Burlamacco and we also love paper, so it comes naturally to make a paper version of Burlamacco.

Creating Burlabox, we have simplified the shape of Burlamacco with an essential volume, ensuring recognizability of the character, with a papertoy that's easy to make, even for children.

Quoting Bruno Munari: "Progress means simplifying, not complicating. Complicating is easy; simplifying is difficult. Removing instead of adding means acknowledging the essence of things and communicating it in their essentiality."

Burlabox is quite the world traveler. What are some of your favorite places he has visited?

Burlabox is a free spirit and he loves to be photographed around the world. Sometimes we receive photos of his travels, but we don't always know where he is exactly. Among his many trips, real and virtual, we think the most interesting was when he had been in space without gravity and then he discovered that nothing is like home!

What is it that you love about paper?

We love the ephemeral lightness of the paper and its manifold freedom of expression. So far, we have experienced the use of paper in many situations: micro architectures, installations, books and, finally, a papertoy. We think that paper is a material rich in history and is still a part of our life and our culture.

Why do you think Burlamacco is still so popular today? What is the secret of his longevity?

Burlamacco is a way of life. He's never too serious, and he takes everything with a smile. Burlamacco faces all the events of politics and society with irony, but without forgetting that under his immense and radiant smile there is a man with all his doubts and his pain. Burlamacco is a mask that communicates to us a very important message: We can change many things in the world without lamenting, but smiling.

Can you tell us a little more about the carnival of Viareggio?

The carnival of Viareggio is the most famous carnivalesque event in Italy and one of the most important of Europe, recalling hundreds of thousands of visitors from all over the world. The Viareggio carnival was born in 1873 as a folk event. And at present, it can be considered as a dynamic and lively show, which attracts to itself the attention of Italian and international medias, besides a large audience composed of people of every age.

The stars of these spectacular shows are the huge papier-mâché floats and puppets along the sea promenade in the weeks preceding Easter, offering a wide program of entertainment and fun. The floats, which are in friendly competition for several cups, are manufactured by great craftsmen who are masters of papier-mâché modeling, and feature satiric interpretations of the most recent national and international events.

Politicians, as well as artists and sportsmen, are often recognizable in the characters on the floats, which almost come to life during the parade by the moving arms, opening and closing mouths and rolling eyes. Noteworthy is the program of related events, including a large number of shows and cultural events such as fun, musical comedies in vernacular, festivals, an International Soccer Tournament Carnival Cup and many celebrations.

What inspires you?

Celebrating the carnival means to preserve childhood inside for all your own life. Keep the curiosity to know, the pleasure of understanding, the desire to communicate.

Any words of wisdom from Burlabox?

He who despises masks understands little, or nothing at all. He flees the truth, because life is a carnival.

1. Prescore all dotted fold lines by gently running a craft knife down a straight edge.

2. Cut out.

3. Fold and glue.

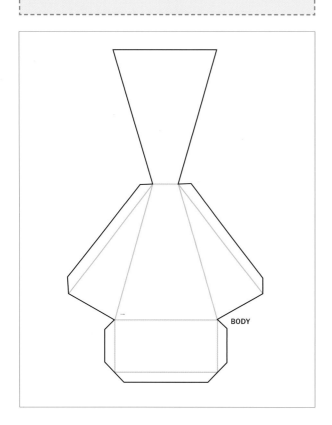

BODY

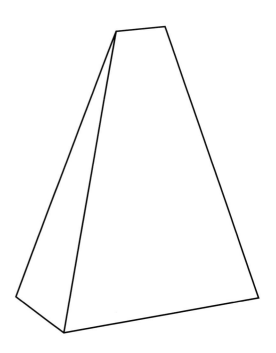

burlabox

atelier
alessio
blanco

burlabox.altervista.org

No. 10 **THUG**

by Filippo Perin, a.k.a. PHIL
Conegliano, Veneto, Italy

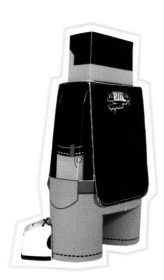

What inspired you to start making papertoys?

Good question. Truly, I do not know why I started. For fun, I think, to test how far I could go. Well, I must thank Shin Tanaka. After seeing his site, I wanted to try making papertoys.

After some collaborations, I decided to try to design my own papertoy, a toy that represented me and that represented the culture that has influenced my art. To create a new toy, I always think until I find the right character to create, a character that embodies itself and also aspects of my personality. Almost my alter ego. I believe that among all the toys I've designed, the G-BOY most reflects my personality. It was the first true papertoy to have meaning for me, and I wanted it to somehow have characteristics similar to mine, which reflect street art and hip-hop culture. It helps me a lot to work to draft a papertoy, and every day is a source of inspiration. The thing I hate, however, is that I have little time to devote to this art because of my work, but I try to always make it better.

What advantages do you see with paper over other materials, such as vinyl or plush?

I do not see significant technical benefits, but it is certainly the most recyclable material. But thinking of the advantages there are, paper has a low price, is readily available, and having it applied to toys makes it even more special. The paper makes the toy unique in all its forms. Even if the design is the same, all its copies will be unique, even if just for small details. Each papertoy is born to become the limited edition of itself! The

fortune, but also perhaps misfortune, of papertoys is that they are not in stores, except a few exceptions, and I think that their value exceeds that of any other toy on the market. At least as far as I am concerned, in my toys, I put my soul and passion, love, hate—I put part of me in each of them, and they reflect my emotions. The paper is life!

What has been your experience selling your papertoys?

It was a short experience! I did two series of ten pieces each for a store in Rome and one in my town. It was interesting, and I realized that something was changing in Italy, the way people viewed their world. In fact, the first set sold out! Now, I am not interested in taking other series to be sold because I want my toys to maintain a more artistic value, to be noncommercial.

And this is what the movement of designer toys should be.

What advice would you give people who want to design their own papertoys?

Start from simple shapes, and then switch to increasingly complex ones. This helps you choose your own style in the construction of the toy. Do not start with ambitious projects, but with projects that are simple and linear and perhaps original.

How do you go about designing a new papertoy?

Step by step, keeping styles and forms that have already been tested. In my case, I spend a lot of time drafting the model, because not using programs for the design, I have to study the shapes very carefully. This takes one or two months. But once you get a good capacity, you can create the shape of a paper-toy in a few hours. The time it took me to realize my Thug toy was only two hours. Incredible. Switching from an old design to a new design means, however, starting from the beginning. I retain the physical characteristics specific to each toy, but I want each one to have its own personality and a unique design.

Can you tell us about your recent feature on MTV?

They contacted me to show the world of papertoys to all of Italy. It was a short appearance and a beautiful experience. I hope I can repeat it sooner or later. It certainly gave me a lot of visibility.

How do you tell people about your new work and keep them informed?

I contact all concerned by e-mail and MySpace. I do not have a mailing list, but I'm creating one. Now I have hundreds of contacts, and I am glad to see that many people consult my MySpace page for information.

What's next for PHIL? Any cool projects on the horizon?

I have some projects in mind. Thanks to my last collaboration, I came into contact with a large sportswear company that asked me to work at the launch of some of its products. But my collaborations with the world of urban culture will continue forever because it is a world that I much respect.

Can papertoys save the world?

Yes, they will save it. Papertoys are fortunate enough to be a product very simple to build. And they are not objects intended for an elite people—they are meant for all. In the coming months, I'm working on another project for children, especially those who are less fortunate. We say that, in this case, the papertoys are already helping the world to be better.

1. Prescore all fold lines by gently running a craft knife down a straight edge.

2. Cut out all objects. Be sure to cut the red lines and the black lines on PANTS so edges can be rolled.

3. Fold and glue HEAD together.

4. Fold and glue the SHIRT together.

5. Glue SHOES together, then fold up and glue them to PANTS.

6. Roll and glue pant LEGS.

7. Tuck ARMS in pants and SHIRT tails outside pants and glue in place.

8. Glue HEAD to top of SHIRT where marked.

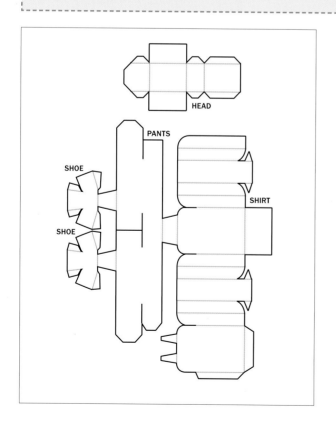

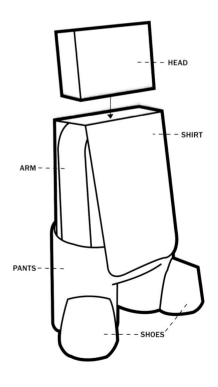

PAPER TOY BOOK

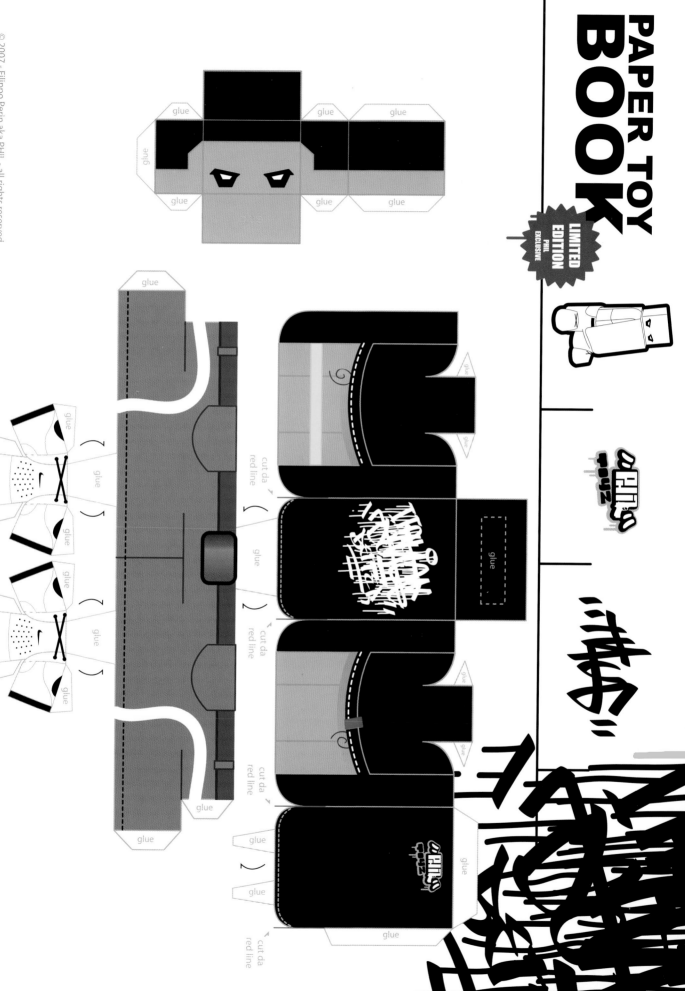

LIMITED EDITION PHIL EXCLUSIVE

What do you think is paper's biggest advantage over vinyl and plush?

I think that the ability to instantly put them in people's hands all over the world is pretty advantageous. Not to mention being able to make them free. Designer toys for everyone! Nice.

What do you see in the future for designer papertoys?

I think this book is a very good start. But I guess we'll just have to wait and see what's next!

1. Prescore all fold lines by gently running a craft knife down a straight edge.

2. Cut out all objects. Be sure to cut slots in HANDS for holding SPEAR and TORCH and slot above eyes on HEAD for KEY.

3. Glue TORCH and SPEAR front to back.

4. Glue HANGER to back of MASK.

5. Glue HANG TAB on ARM front to back.

6. Fold and glue LEGS, ARMS, HEAD and BODY.

7. Glue penny to bottom of BODY where marked.

8. Glue ANKLE SHIRTS into rings and slip onto LEGS. Glue LEGS onto BODY.

9. Glue ARMS and HEAD onto BODY.

10. Slip KEY through HANGER on MASK and into slot on HEAD.

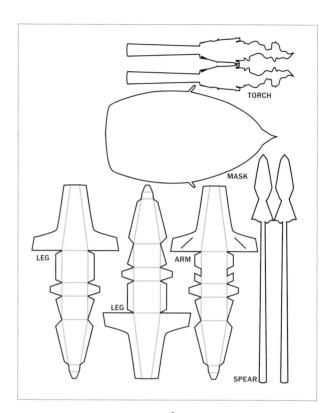

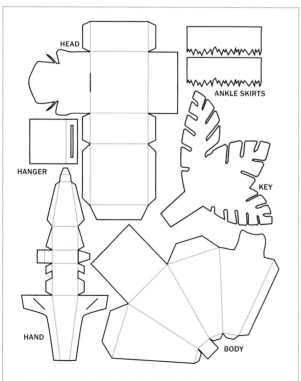

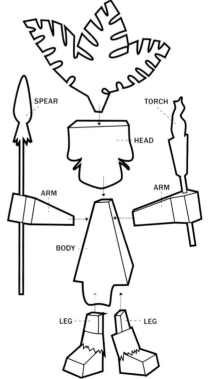

Freaky Tiki
by NiceBunny™

© Brian Castleforte 2007
www.nicebunny.com

(Back view)
Hang shield
from HANG
TAB on hand

(Back view)
Slide the KEY into the
KEYTAB to attach shield as mask

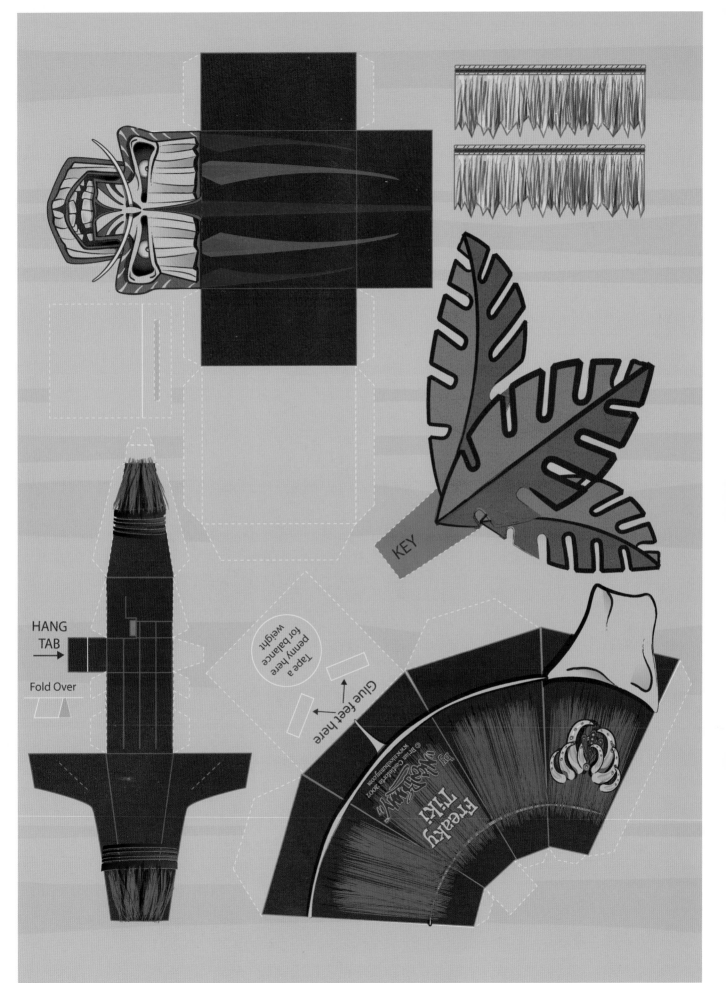

HANG
TAB

Fold Over

Tape a
penny here
for balance
weight

Glue feet here

KEY

Freaky Tiki
by ...
www.creaturekat.com 2007

No. 12 **REDY**

by Angello Garcîa Bassi, a.k.a. Cubotoy
Antofagasta, Chile

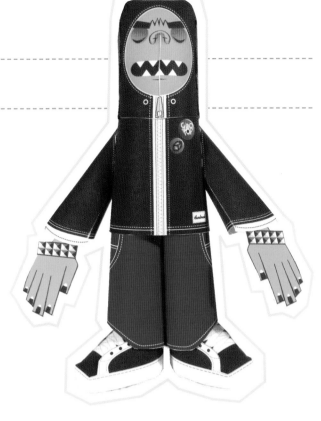

What inspired you to start making papertoys?

My interest in making these toys was born when I became aware of Art Toy. This type of underground art is being experienced by many artists around the world…just a look at the Internet is enough to realize this. Well, among the infinite number of answers developed in all types of material, I found one that attracted my attention a lot: the work based on origami, which uses paper as its basic material.

These toys are born of a number of concepts, and the main premise was to seek a new platform or surface on which to design. The best way was by means of something less costly than vinyl, and something that was easy to recognize. And so the idea of mixing the classic Japanese technique of origami with designs influenced by pop culture and street art was born.

What was the first Cubotoy you designed? Do you have a favorite Cubotoy?

The first papertoy I designed was E-Mouth, then later E-Moe… these two characters were the ones that encouraged me to design more and more models and to create my brand, Cubotoy.

Each piece, each arm and track shoe is made by me. All of the work is developed manually by two hands, ten fingers, a head and a lot of interest! For that reason, I don't have only one favorite. Each Cubotoy means something very special to me. I feel strongly about all of them, and they all have something that makes them my favorite.

I love the googly eyes on your toys. Where did you get that idea from?

As my toys are made of paper—and, in a way, are static—I needed a way to make them more expressive…and the idea of putting moving eyes on them gave excellent results. It gives them a certain life that other toys don't have.

How long does it take for you to build a Cubotoy?

Each Cubotoy means a different assembly time. Some with more simplified forms, such as Zeta, take me around two hours, but others, like J-Fox, take an average of three hours to put together.

How many toys have you made so far?

To date, I have designed fourteen characters, but I have seven more soon to be released.

Do you find that people are receptive to a toy made of paper?

From the start, people showed interest in Cubotoys; first, because they are made of paper, and second, due to the different and complex shapes that can be obtained by just cutting, folding and pasting.

The plastic aspect of Cubotoys and their moving eyes make one forget momentarily that they are made of paper. And the fact that they are dressed with clothing for youths allows the spectator to identify with and to feel a greater appreciation for my characters.

What does the future hold for Cubotoy? Any cool projects in the works?

The future of Cubotoy is uncertain. I just enjoy creating each toy and, if it were up to me, I would like to consolidate myself as a toy designer right now.

Among the future projects I have in mind, there is one that motivates me more than the rest. This has to do with the creation of a band of virtual musicians with Cubotoy characters, with which I am currently developing music and videos to promote them. This project is very interesting and valuable, and the best part is that each music CD will be attached to the toy box for each band.

What advice would you give someone who wanted to start designing papertoys?

That with perseverance, working with paper has no limits. If you have a good idea, cut, fold and paste until you do it.

When you're not hard at work making Cubotoys what are you up to?

I work as a publicity graphic designer, and as a professor at the university where I studied.

If you had to sum up Cubotoy in a few words, what would it be?

Infinite possibilities.

---

1. Prescore all fold lines by gently running a craft knife down a straight edge.

2. Cut out all objects.

3. Fold and glue HANDS front to back and trim off excess.

4. Fold and glue HEAD.

5. Glue TORSO into cylinder.

6. Roll and glue LEGS into tubes.

7. Build SHOES and roll and glue SOCKS.

8. Fold and glue ARMS, and glue onto TORSO where marked.

9. Glue HANDS inside the ARMS.

10. Slip HEAD over and down on top of TORSO.

11. Slide LEGS inside TORSO.

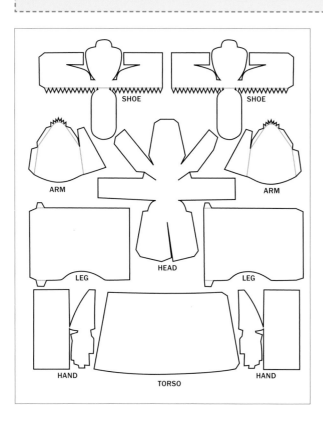

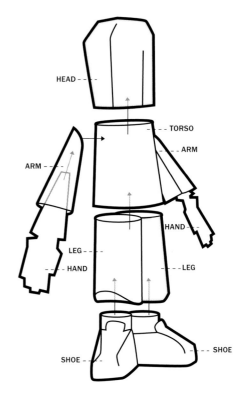

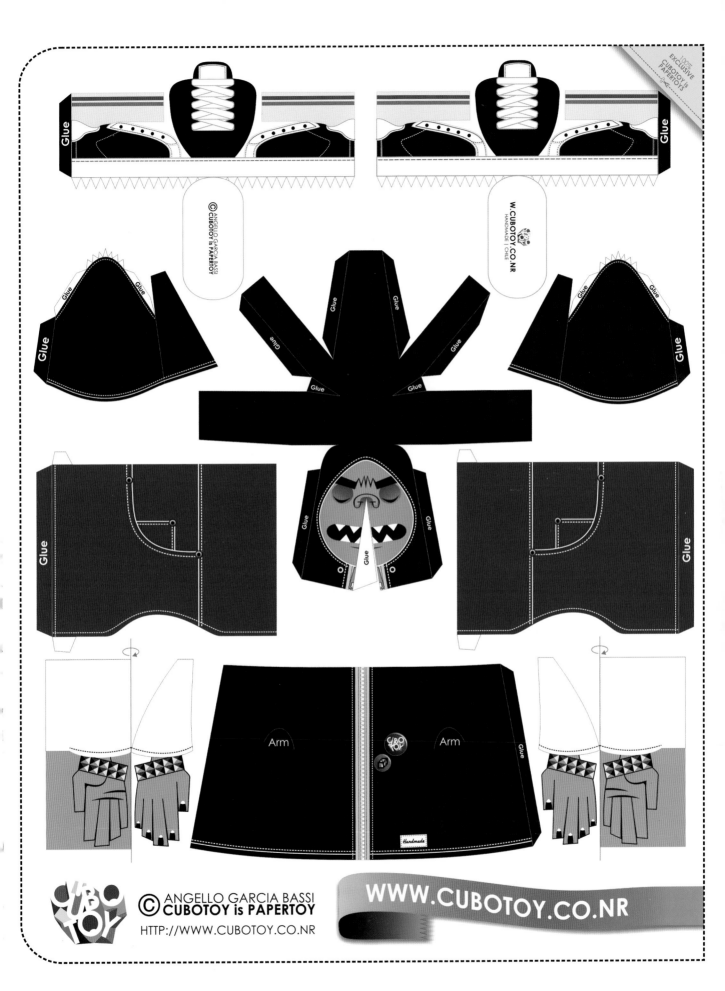

No. 13 FELTY BOY

by Jerom
Dijon, France

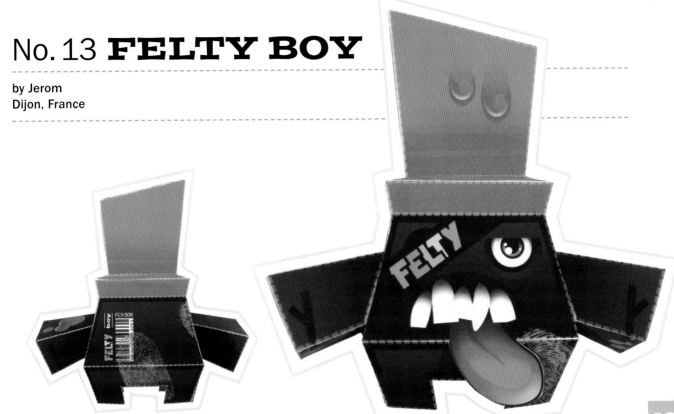

Why paper? What was it that got you interested in making papertoys?

It was about February 2007, with Fwis's Readymechs. (I found them cute and original.) Then I threw myself in it. It seemed easy, new and pretty cool to make. And it seemed more fun than traditional origami stuff. Then, it allowed me to use the vectorial tool on my computer, which I used only a little before. I've been drawing for some years, using the computer as a sidekick for colorizing, in particular.

You might be one of the most prolific papertoy designers I know. How many toys have you designed?

All in all, I've done about fourteen papertoys, created over ten months; besides that, I have about fifteen toys waiting for achievement. Some of them take me weeks to achieve. I focus too much on the template, the accessories, or I find them not as good as I expected and I wait for a better approach. But sometimes, some are clinched in one evening! Well, it's kind of variable.

What advantages does paper have over other materials like plush or vinyl?

For me, it's easier to directly create a papertoy (the patterns I create are not that complex, you know…) than make or customize real art toyz! Besides that, most papertoys are free, and the medium is easy to propagate.

What are some of the most challenging things about papertoy design?

The most complex part is the template, how to assemble the different facets of the papertoy. Well, I have to admit that I don't really have problems with conceiving my papertoys. In my opinion, these are very simple patterns. There are no animated mechanisms, complicated shapes, etc. But even this part of the work is fun. The most laborious task is to add indications and the dotted lines—forget creativity!

I couldn't agree more! What advice would you give someone who wanted to start designing papertoys?

To start, my advice is to take a simple geometric figure—a cube, a pyramid, a parallelepiped—to learn where to place facets and how to sketch designs on a flattened 3-D object.

Can you tell us a little about how you approach designing a papertoy?

To choose the subject of my next papertoy…well, I don't really have a method. Inspiration comes from one of my drawings, or from a picture seen somewhere else that makes me want to build the global idea in 3-D—that's how I started the Paperbanana, Djala, the Supermariocubes, the Onigiri. Alternatively, I start from a geometric figure and I imagine what could pop out of it. An animal? A character? After some rough sketches, to figure out the final aspect and the template, I start Photoshop, and the papertoy comes to life! I use the pen tool and some textures. I can make it straight off (in one evening, a weekend, or a few days), or I build it progressively: I add faces, I change the size, I add some decoration, etc. It can be laborious!

What is your most popular papertoy?

The Papersushi pair—so easy to build, and so kawaii!

What are some of your other interests besides papertoys?

I always had a passion for comics (European, American or Asiatic), and one of these days, I hope I will finish my own comic book! Besides comics, I cultivate a fascination for toyz—street culture in general (graffiti, design, etc.). I'm not born in that universe, but the creativity that springs out of all this culture is marvelous, inspiring and enthusiastic!

What do you do for a living?

Alas, my creations don't pay the rent. I still have my student job, in a shoe boutique!

Have you ever suffered a paper cut while working on your papertoys?

Not yet!

What was your inspiration for Felty Boy, the papertoy in this book?

I wanted to make a character more stylish, more complex than usual. And, if you want to customize a toy, to choose a character with a big head is always a good idea! And for an anecdote, Posca, a heavy gouache felt-tip pen, was one of my favorite art tools. There was a time when I used only this!

---

1. Prescore all fold dotted lines by gently running a craft knife down a straight edge.

2. Cut out all objects. Be sure to cut a hole in the top of BODY.

3. Fold and glue FELT TIP together. Poke through the hole in the top of BODY and glue tabs on FELT TIP to the inside of the BODY.

4. Fold and glue HANDS.

5. Glue hand tabs inside body.

6. Finish glueing body together.

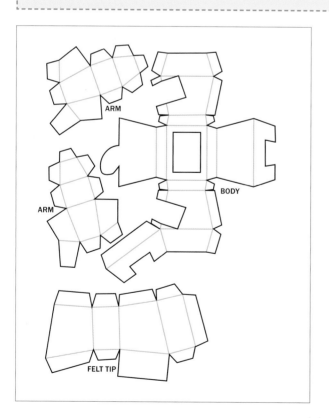

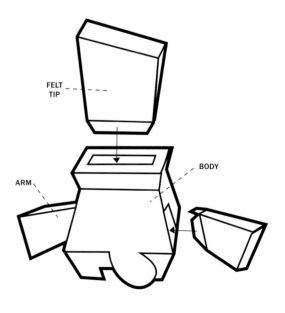

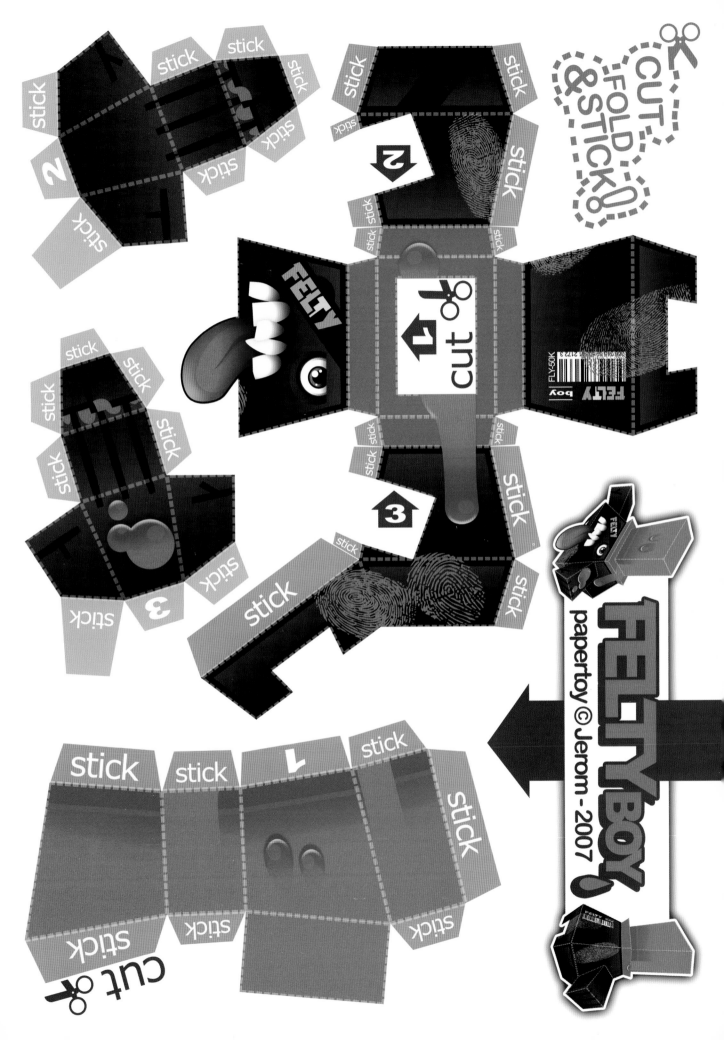

No. 14 NANIDAD AND THE PEEPS

by mckibillo
Chigasaki, Japan

What inspired you to start the NaniBird papertoy project?

A couple of things. First, the work of Ben the Illustrator really inspired me. It was so cool seeing how he allowed and promoted his Speakerdog as a platform for all the really amazing designs that got submitted. It just seemed like such a fun way to collaborate with a bunch of people. Also, I had initially thought of it as a way to promote a series of paintings I did last year. I'd made a hundred paintings of birds all asking "nani" or "what" in Japanese, which pretty much reflects my daily experience of living here. But that quickly fell to the wayside as I got more into the paper crafting itself. The NaniBird papertoy is definitely its own creature now.

Where did you live before Japan?

We moved to Japan in 2004 straight from Brooklyn, New York, so it was a pretty big shift. In many ways I'm still adjusting to life here.

What is your favorite thing about paper as a medium?

It's so cheap!

What is your least favorite thing about it?

It's not so great for curved shapes.

How did you go about designing the form for NaniBird?

Trial and error, really. I didn't use any kind of 3-D program or anything. I first sketched out the basic shape, and then refined what was possible to build by refining the final form using Illustrator. I went through a few different variations until I got something that could be built and still look somewhat like a bird. The important thing for me was keeping the profile shape, the silhouette. That's the thing I started with.

How did you get the word out about the NaniBird project?

Through a few different web sites…through www.nanibird.com, of course, as well as my blog on www.drawger.com. I also posted announcements on The Little Chimp Society (http://thelittlechimpsociety.com) and notcot.org. And I e-mailed everyone I knew asking for submissions. After a while, it just got picked up and made a run around the 'net, getting mentioned by various blogs and sites.

There are a lot of cool designs in series one. Do you have a favorite?

Oh, that's a tough question. Well, out of deference to all the great designers and artists who have contributed and are still submitting designs, I'd have to say I love them all. Lame, I know, but it's true!

Do you know which NaniBird has been downloaded the most?

No, I don't really have the site set up for it.

How does this project tie in with the rest of your work?

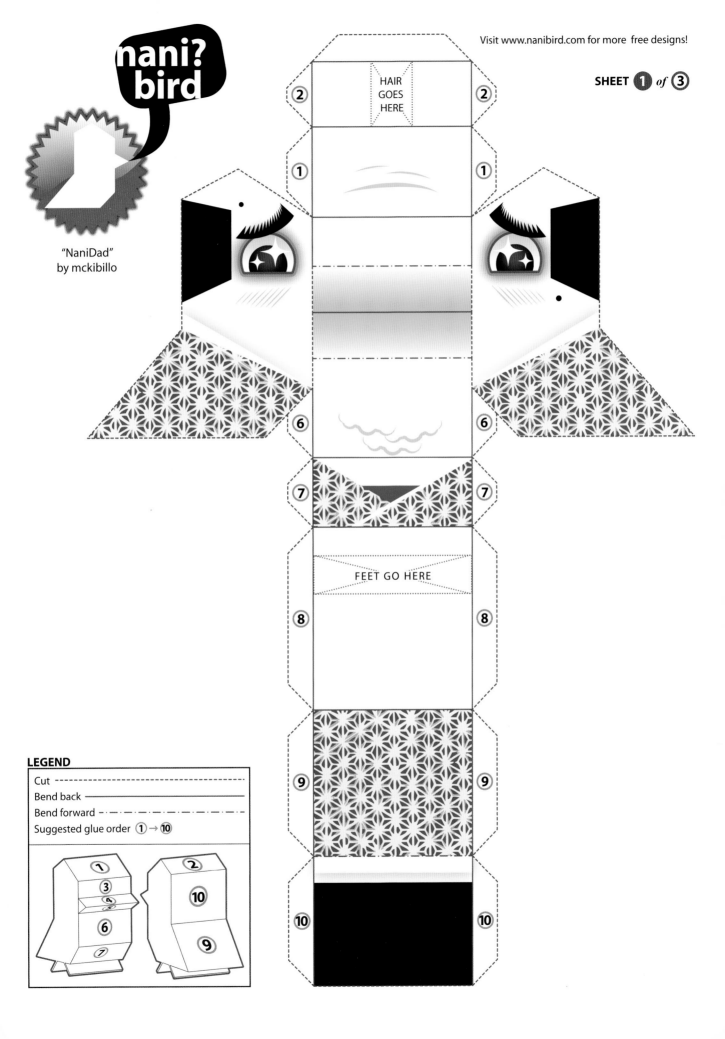

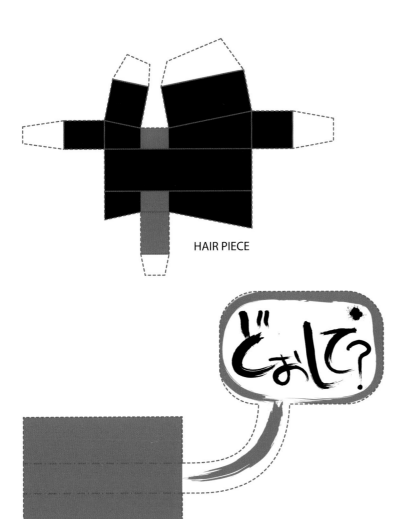

HAIR PIECE

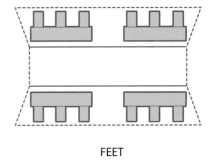

FEET

SPEECH BUBBLE

TIPS

1) Use thick paper, the thicker the better.

2) After glueing down the head flaps, glue the SPEECH BUBBLE to the inside of the beak **before** moving on to the rest of the body.

3) To increase the stability of your birdie tape a coin to the **inside** of the bottom flap (where the feet go).

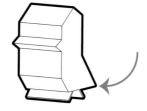

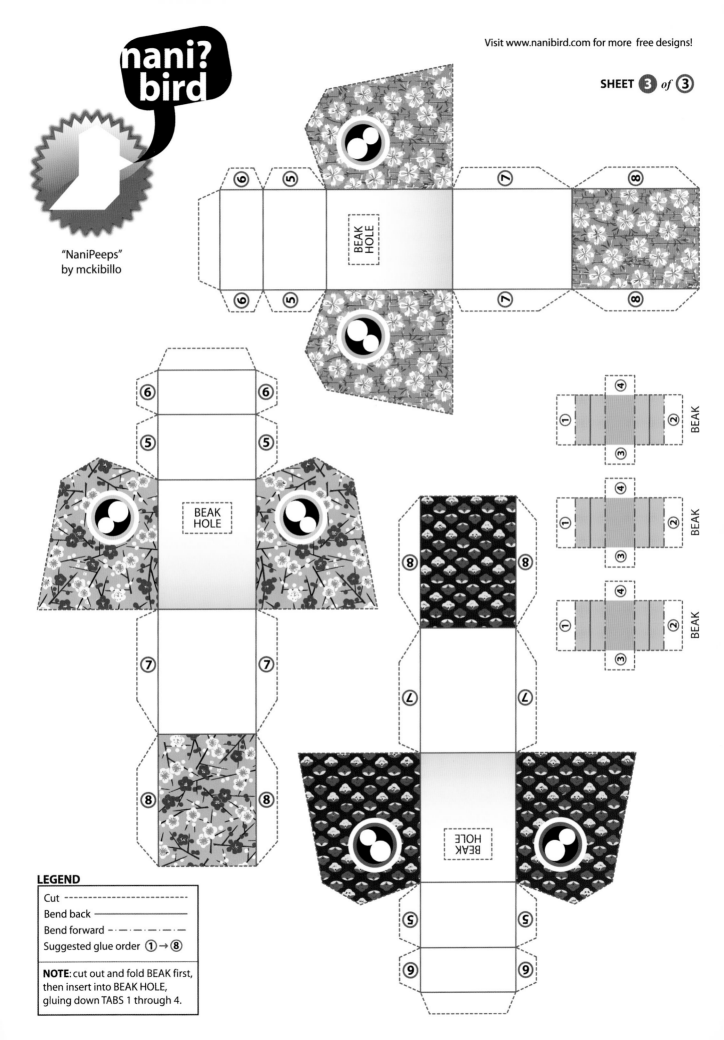

No. 15 **HOTROD DOGBUG**

by Sjors Trimbach
Enschede, The Netherlands

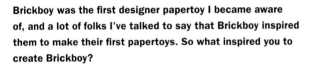

Brickboy was the first designer papertoy I became aware of, and a lot of folks I've talked to say that Brickboy inspired them to make their first papertoys. So what inspired you to create Brickboy?

A really boring meeting.

I'm always drawing and doodling in meetings at my work to stay awake, and in this one I drew a character that was made of square parts, like pixels. I thought it would be easy to make on a computer with 3-D software. Since I don't know how to work with 3-D programs, I ended up doing it "analog" and made a paper prototype, just to see how it could look in 3-D. This turned into Brickboy, a name I had used for an earlier character that was basically a brick with a face. When I was about ready to show it on a message board, I saw Kenn Munk with his Antlors and knew I wasn't the only one going the paper way. His work gave me a small push to go on.

Was Brickboy your first papertoy experience?

I had made some Christmas cards with parts that you could cut out and put together to make a small diorama, but besides that, I didn't have any experience making papertoys. It's quite easy, actually…well, mostly.

What was the most challenging part of bringing Brickboy into the world?

Getting the proportions correct. Most features were sketched out, and somehow I managed to make him stand in one go. But making him look good took quite a few prototypes.

What advantages do you think papertoys have over vinyl or plush toys?

People can print them on cheap paper so it looks crappy, people can have huge fingers and half crush your design, glue can be smeared all over it, printer ink can run or get spotty, and they can misinterpret your instructions and build the model wrong. All stuff you obviously don't have when giving people a readymade vinyl or plush toy.

But I make them because I can start a sketch in the morning and have a full 3-D toy in my hands in the evening. I love to think about the best way to build it, how to design it, how to avoid difficult shapes or how to make difficult shapes. It takes time and effort to make a good paper model. If you want, you can produce and distribute them for free through the Internet and have your toys all over the world in no time. Basically, anyone can do it. That is also a bit of a problem; since anyone and his mother can put a paper model on their sites, there's lots of crap out there. Most of them are Readymech rip-offs. Paper models are cool because you can make whatever you want without a company telling you what is "hot" or what will sell.

I don't know much about the process of making toys other than papertoys. All I can say is that I am working with a company on a vinyl figure and after almost a year, as far as I know, nothing has happened.

Paper seems pretty instant, I'm sure, compared to the process of getting a vinyl toy made. What do you think makes a successful papertoy design?

I think it's two things: One, the figure, the design (a monkey, a robot, or whatever) and two, the level of skills needed to build it. I've seen amazing paper battleships that need at least five years of technical engineering skills to build, so only two people have tried it. My Brickboys have some great designs and are fairly easy to build, so they are quite successful, if I may say so. Just as with all toys, it starts with a good idea or character. With papertoys, you also need to make sure people can build it.

What are you working on now? Any cool projects in the works? I've heard rumors floating around about a new Brickboy series.

I am always working on too many things and never have enough time to finish them. I have some illustrations lying around that I want to ink and color, there's a custom toy or three that I need to finish (one person has been waiting for over a year!), I have made a new paper model that I need to find a place for, the BS model needs work, my 500+ Christmas MP3 collection needs some updating, I have plans for new Badgers and, yes, the Brickboy overhaul that has been planned for years. At this moment, I have closed it for new entries, and I am very sorry about that. Someday I will find the time (and inspiration!) to breathe new life into my boy.

But my main project, which I really can't wait to start on, is a wooden figure. Wood is the new paper.

---

1. Prescore all dotted fold lines by gently running a craft knife down a straight edge.

2. Cut out all objects. Be sure to cut a tongue slot on INSIDE OF MOUTH and cut and remove the mouth piece on BODY labeled CUT OUT!

3. Fold BODY and glue tabs to make BODY box.

4. Insert TONGUE and glue into slot in the middle of INSIDE OF MOUTH. Fold INSIDE OF MOUTH into C shape. Insert

into mouth of BODY and glue front side of tabs inside BODY to form the inside of the mouth.

5. Glue RIGHT and LEFT EAR into pyramids and glue on top of BODY where marked.

6. Glue FRONT and BACK FEET into boxes and glue to bottom of BODY where marked.

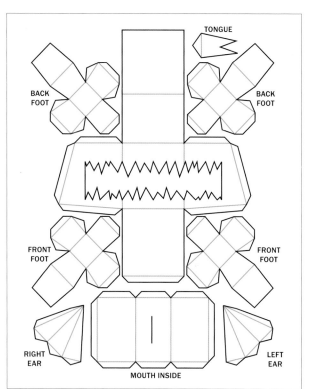

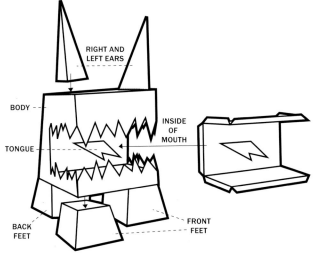

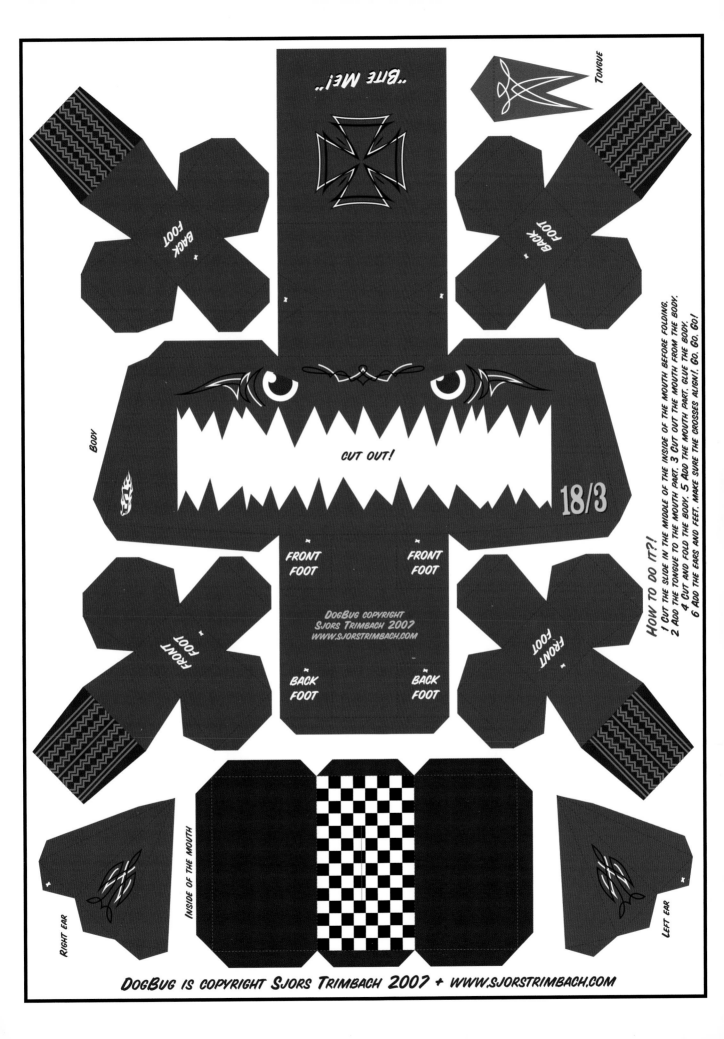

No. 16 **PAPERBOY**

by Marshall Alexander
Arnhem, The Netherlands

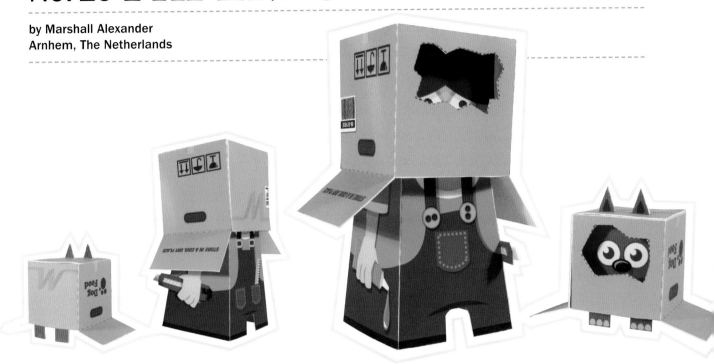

What inspired you to jump into the papertoy arena?

One of the first designer papertoys I encountered was the Readymech series. I'd seen some other styles of paper craft and origami before, but these models showed perfectly how you could use the same concepts that are used for vinyl designer toys, and apply them to a paper model. So that inspired me to give it a go myself. My first papertoy, which was heavily inspired by the Readymech series, got a lot of positive reactions, which prompted me to do some more. What I especially liked was the level of interaction that was created by letting people assemble these toys themselves. I also felt it was similar to those street-art projects where artists leave their work on the streets for everyone to enjoy, which is something that I really connect with. No commercial motives, just doing it for fun.

A monkey astronaut, a biohazard dude, a monster from the muddy waters, and a shark attack. What's next?

I feel I am still in the early stages of discovering papertoy design, so it is hard to tell. I keep a sketchbook and a folder on my Mac that I use to gather ideas, sketches and reference material, and I also play around with blank paper in order to come up with new ways to fold a model. My inspiration mainly comes from animated movies, games, toys and comics, so my papertoys usually are characters with some kind of backstory I've made up. I want people to look at the toy and wonder who he is and what he has been up to. What I still would like to do is a whole set piece with multiple characters and props as well. But my short attention span will probably keep me from ever completing such a thing.

Sounds like quite the project. What are some of the movies, comics and things that inspire you?

I'm a big fan of animated movies in all its appearances, ranging from the Disney classics to the work from Studio Ghibli, Aardman and Pixar, so I get a lot of ideas out of those. Growing up in Europe, I was not really into American comics. Instead, I read Hergé's Tintin and Franquin's Gaston Lagaffe until the books basically fell apart. What fascinates me is how these animators and artists manage to take material like pixels, clay or ink and bring it to life in such a way that you get completely absorbed in the world and characters they have created. I'd love to be able to achieve the same in my own work. Illustration-wise, I get my inspiration from basically everywhere. I'm always collecting interesting illustrations and pictures and sticking them into this big scrapbook. When I'm in need of some ideas, I flip through it to get the creative juices in my brain going. In general, I'm interested in things like street art, vintage toys and video games, art deco architecture, pop art, zombies, robots, sci-fi and the list goes on and on. I guess somehow all these interests are reflected in my work, although I find it hard to pinpoint where, exactly.

What do you think are some of the advantages that papertoys have over vinyl or plush toys?

OK, this sounds like a good time to do some serious papertoy promotion. First of all, there is, of course, the interactive experience you create. There's nothing more fun than knowing people download your model, print it out, construct it with nothing more than a knife and some glue, and therefore are an active part of the creation of the model. And sometimes they even send you a picture of the end result. How great is that? Then there's the logistic advantage as well. If you have a digital version of your model, you can easily distribute it over the Internet to all the corners of the world, no shipping costs. Most papertoys are available for free, which means more people will get it and actually build it. For me personally, there's also the practical advantage that papertoys perfectly fit into the method I use to create my other work as well. I usually create my 2-D work in Illustrator. I'm a control freak and like to have control over every little line I draw, and I can keep this control when I design papertoys as well. Finally, although it may not be an advantage over vinyl or plush, it is just plain fun to design papertoys, and I recommend that everyone has a go at it. You can always start with some customs first, and then move on to completely designing your own toys. Just enjoy!

Right on. Can you tell us a little bit about your project for this book, Paperboy? Who is he? What drives him? And who is his little friend?

Since I decided to do a special papertoy exclusive to this book, I thought it would be fun to do a papertoy that somehow refers to art of making papertoys itself. So I made up Paperboy, a little boy who's crazy about the papertoys his dad creates. He loves them so much, he decides he wants to be one himself. He then grabs some old cardboard boxes, a knife and some glue and starts building. Unfortunately, his pet (of a currently undefined New Guinea species) unwillingly has to participate in the project as well. It's not until he gets to eat the whole content of a box full of dog food in order to empty it that he's happy to walk around with a piece of cardboard on his head. And that's what Paperboy is about. I hope you all like him. So get your knives and glue out and start building.

1. Prescore all dotted fold lines by gently running a craft knife down a straight edge.

2. Cut out all objects. Be sure to cut holes in front of BOXES and ear holes in top of dog's BOX.

3. Fold and glue KNIFE front to back.

4. Glue tab to form boy's BODY.

5. Fold and glue boy's BOX.

6. Slip boy's FACE into box so eyes are visible.

7. Fold and glue dog's EARS and FEET front to back.

8. Slip dog's EARS through slots in top of BOX.

9. Glue dog's BOX together.

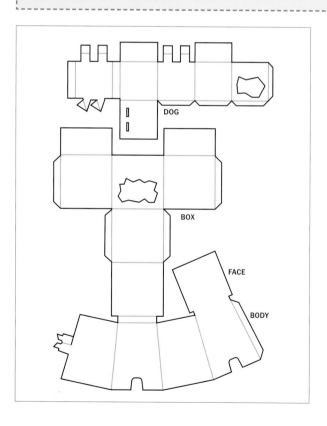

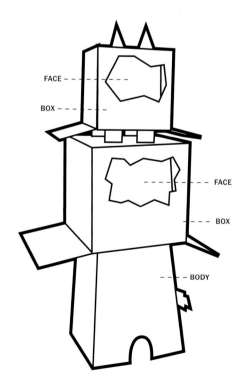

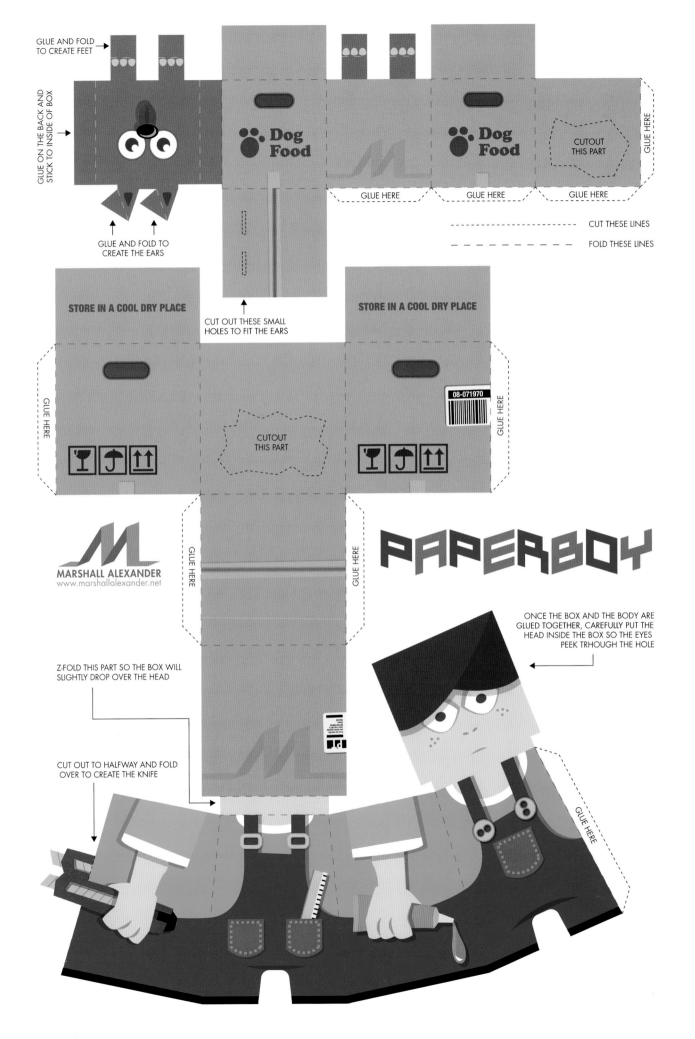

GLUE AND FOLD
TO CREATE FEET

GLUE ON THE BACK AND
STICK TO INSIDE OF BOX

GLUE AND FOLD TO
CREATE THE EARS

Dog Food

Dog Food

CUTOUT
THIS PART

GLUE HERE

GLUE HERE   GLUE HERE   GLUE HERE

GLUE HERE

-          CUT THESE LINES

-          FOLD THESE LINES

STORE IN A COOL DRY PLACE

STORE IN A COOL DRY PLACE

CUT OUT THESE SMALL
HOLES TO FIT THE EARS

GLUE HERE

GLUE HERE

08-071970

CUTOUT
THIS PART

MARSHALL ALEXANDER
www.marshallalexander.net

GLUE HERE

GLUE HERE

PAPERBOY

ONCE THE BOX AND THE BODY ARE
GLUED TOGETHER, CAREFULLY PUT THE
HEAD INSIDE THE BOX SO THE EYES
PEEK TRHOUGH THE HOLE

Z-FOLD THIS PART SO THE BOX WILL
SLIGHTLY DROP OVER THE HEAD

CUT OUT TO HALFWAY AND FOLD
OVER TO CREATE THE KNIFE

GLUE HERE

No. 17 GO BANANAS

by Horrorwood
Takamatsu, Japan

What inspired you to start making papertoys?

I am an avid toy collector and have always wanted to create my own toys. Unfortunately, I am not that adept at handicraft and the like, and so paper craft provided me with a way to bring my artwork into the 3-D realm. Luckily, most of my artwork takes the form of simple character design and I produce it digitally, so it was not a big leap to turn my work into paper form. I produced a set of very simple block toys about three years ago. My first character was called Blocula and was, unsurprisingly, a cube-based Dracula. After that, for some reason, I kind of left it for a while.

However, last year I noticed that paper craft seemed to be booming, and I felt inspired to start creating again. I really like the idea that people can come to my web site and go away with something tangible, and it is a great way for artists like me to promote their work.

How do you approach designing a new papertoy?

I have an ideas book in which I sketch down the basic idea for each toy, and then work out how and whether the piece will work in 3-D and flat form. As I am a little impatient with most of my work, after a quick sketch, I go straight into Illustrator to lay down the basic framework and measure all the dimensions so I can get started with the fun part—the artwork. I don't usually do a dry run to make sure that the figure will work, so I have been very lucky so far to find that all of my toys have worked straight off when I first printed them out and assembled them.

I like the toy to look appealing in 2-D form, and some people I give my toys to actually keep it like that without cutting it out, which I find quite flattering. I also like to create toys that people can actually "play" with, with removable and movable parts and the like. I am the kind of toy collector who actually opens the box and plays around with my figures, and I try to carry this ethic through into my paper craft.

What advice would you give to people who want to design their own papertoys?

Start with something simple in form, and then build up to more complex structures. Think about the constraints of the medium and try to work around them. As with plastic toys, keeping the artwork simple is also a good idea, in my mind. Look at other artists' paper work and see what forms and designs look best. Also remember that if you have trouble constructing your own craft, then others probably will, too. Though the aesthetics of the finished product come first, I believe it should be fun and satisfying to make for the consumer. Also (though this is very hypocritical), a construction dry run may be a good idea before going to all the trouble of adding artwork to your toy.

When it comes to the finished piece, personally I try to leave as little blank space as possible. By this, I mean I try to create paper craft that fits together in a way that doesn't reveal the blank side of the paper. I think this is a good discipline and provides a more satisfying finished piece. Finally, though this is an obvious point, working digitally also makes life a lot easier.

What's next? Do you have any cool projects coming up?

Apart from the papertoys, I am really into making T-shirts at present. I recently purchased silkscreen equipment and am slowly learning the art of printing my own shirts. As with paper craft, I feel that T-shirts are a great canvas for artists, and my head is full of possible designs right now. I am also trying to stick with my promise of producing a free paper craft download for my web site each month. I also have an idea for a platform toy that fits together with others in the set, which will be more sci-fi than horror in theme. Ideally, I would love to do some collaborative work with other paper craft artists, too, and I like the idea of a group exhibition.

What inspires you?

Horror, science fiction, nature, myths, legends, Western and Japanese traditions, modern illustration and character design.

Toy design also has a big influence on both my 2-D and 3-D work.

I am also inspired by people around me and by seeing artists who are streets ahead of me in terms of technique and achievements—it pushes me to constantly try to improve my work. When I was doing a dead-end job in London, I was often at a loss for inspiration, but since moving to Japan and being able to enjoy a much freer lifestyle, I find that I have almost too many ideas popping into my head each day, so I guess I am very lucky.

What do you do to pay the bills?

I am currently self-employed and teach English with my wife. A small part of my income comes from art and design work when I can get it. Ideally, I would like to get more work on the design side, but as every artist knows, it is a difficult dream to fulfill.

---

1. Prescore all dotted fold lines by gently running a craft knife down a straight edge.

2. Cut slots in side of HEAD for EARS and around the bottom sides of tires.

3. Insert EAR tabs in slots on HEAD and glue.

4. Glue the top and underside of the cap bill together.

5. Continue gluing tabs to form the rest of HEAD. Close the bottom of HEAD last.

6. Glue top side of BODY to BODY side going down the front and then the LEGS. Close bottom of BODY last.

7. Glue front to back of FEET. Glue FEET on BODY by matching up Xs.

8. Glue HEAD to BODY by matching up Ys. Glue on ARMS by matching up Zs.

9. Glue front to back of WINDSHIELD.

10. Glue tabs around to form front and then rear of TRUCK.

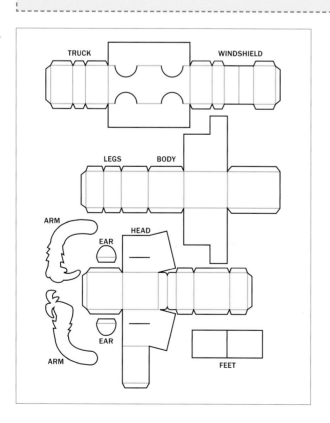

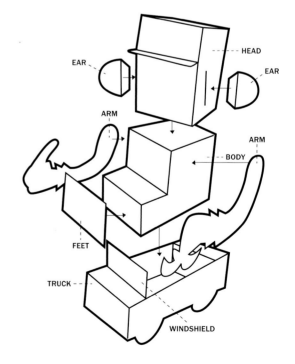

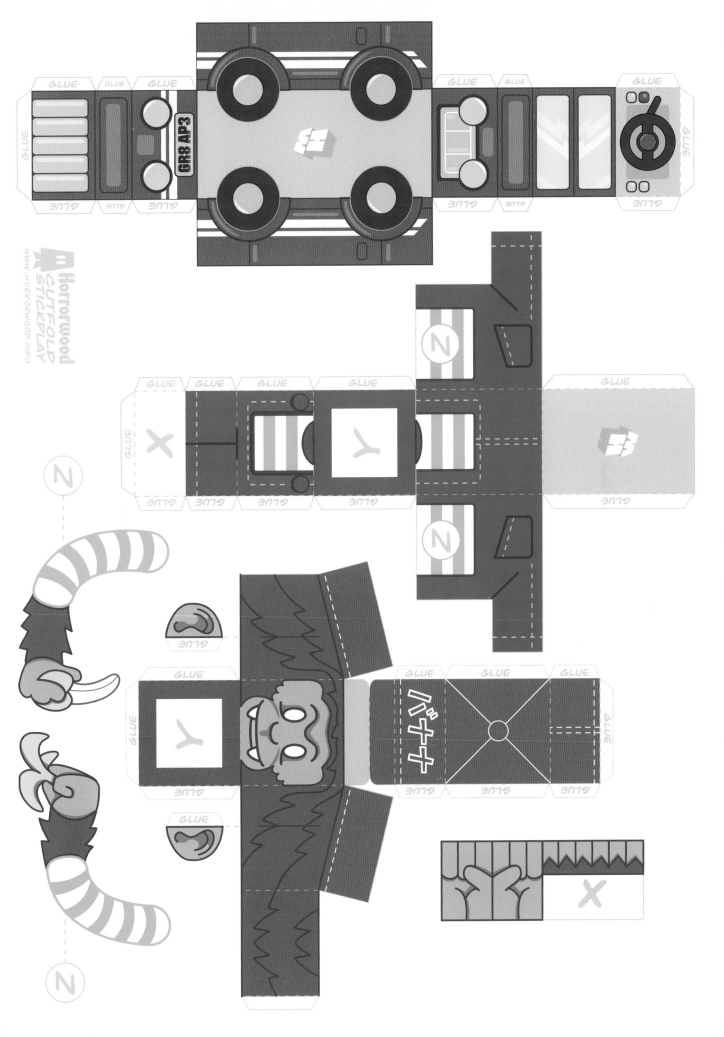

GR8 AP3

No. 18 **BARKLEY**

by Ben the Illustrator
Cornwall, England

So how did you become "Ben the Illustrator"?

I used to work in animation, as creative director of a small animation and design agency. I had a few roles there, not always
creative, plus I was doing illustration jobs on the side.

The illustration jobs were the projects I really put my heart into,
so one day I woke up to the fact, quit my job and walked out of
the studio. I decided to only do the illustration jobs. I decided I
only wanted to be Ben the Illustrator.

So what was your inspiration for Barkley?

I used to do a lot of character illustration, different types of
characters, usually for animation projects—web toons, kids' TV,
advertising, etc.—and I had this method of starting them, when
sketching, where I'd just start drawing a shape, then make it
into a character. Speakerdog pretty much started in the same
way. I wanted something boxy, but with cuteness, so I went for
a boxy-looking dog, then made him into a speaker. I still have
the original sketch of this boxy dog-speaker thing. He had the
speech bubble in that original sketch, but he also had a wire
that connected him to another character. The other character
had a question mark in his speech bubble, like he was asking
a question, and so it progressed. The box-shaped dog had the
exclamation, or the answer. The box-shaped speaker thing was
like a little font of knowledge, or inspiration. He was a speaker,
a dog, a Speakerdog. I got bored of the other character pretty
quickly, started painting canvases with Speakerdog (there is a
canvas somewhere with both characters—that's a one-off for

the history books!), then my buddies took a liking to the canvases, so I started doing more. Speakerdog sat well in beautiful landscapes. It all started coming together, an environmental
aspect, always with a feel-good factor of a billion. So now he's
grown from his humble beginnings to be an environmental mascot, a spokesperson for good times, a little icon with aspira-
tions of bigger and better things, happy times ahead. The more
people got into Speakerdog, the more I wanted to do—tees,
belts, prints, posters, pin badges—then I started getting into
papertoys, so it seemed inevitable. And that pretty much brings
us to today.

What is it about papertoys that appeals to you?

Hard to say! They are so instant: you can draw something, and
suddenly it's a three-dimensional object on your desk. Some
papertoys are beautifully delicate, which is amazing, but I do
prefer chunkier ones. Some people see photos of Speakerdog
papertoys and question whether or not they're vinyl toys. I'm
kind of proud of that, like the fact that the papertoys fool people
into thinking they're vinyl or wood. I also love the whole Internet
phenomenon of it: Put your design on a PDF or something, and
it's anybody's. Just print off the page, and they've got your toy,
free. It was that instant promotional aspect that made me push
the Speakerdogs out into the world. It's a classic craft, but mod-
ernized, adapted for today. It's timeless.

**You have a lot of great custom Speakerdogs on your site by
many talented designers. Was it the idea from the beginning**

to make Speakerdog a platform papertoy for other designers, or did it just kind of develop that way?

It wasn't planned in the beginning, it just kind of happened. I'd designed the papertoy version of Speakerdog because he was getting popular with my illustrations, and I wanted to give people a physical version of him. In the first batch of designs I did, there was The Blank Canvas for people to make their own. I hadn't considered asking other people to get involved at all. Around that time [the end of 2006], I'd designed a Badger papertoy for Sjors Trimbach, and, as far as I remember, it was Sjors's idea to have other people do designs for Speakerdog. And so he did. Sjors delivered a brilliant zombie Speakerdog, and that concreted the concept of having other designers get involved. I sent a bunch of e-mails out to illustrators I already knew, and people whose work I was digging at the time, and sure enough, it all started coming together. We've had some

really great people involved so far, some of my favorite illustrators, like Andrew Groves and Andy Smith, and some artists who were awesome new discoveries for me, who got in touch asking to be involved, like Tsai-Fi and Xuppets. It never fails to surprise me what other people can do with our Speakerdog.

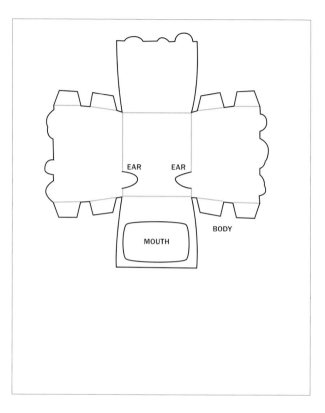

1. Prescore all fold lines by gently running a craft knife down a straight edge.

2. Cut out all objects. Be sure to cut out MOUTH and around the top of EARS.

3. Fold and glue BODY and LEGS.

4. Glue SPEECH BALLOON to BODY.

5. Insert LEGS into BODY.

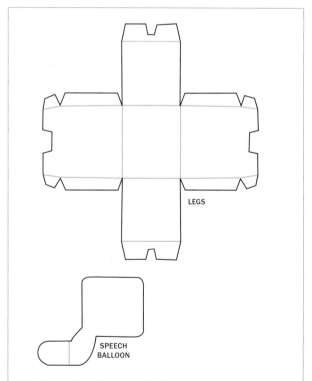

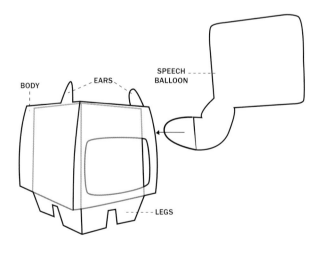

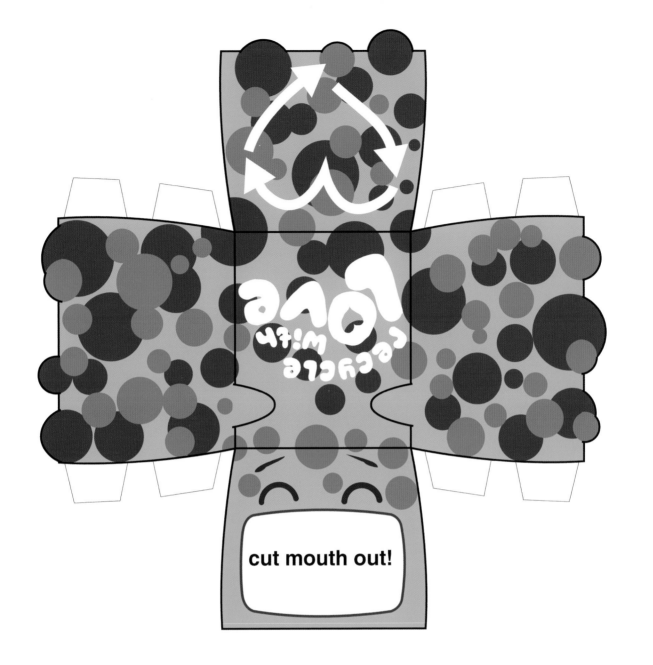

cut mouth out!

"*Barkley*"

An exclusive Speakerdog by Ben the Illustrator

Speakerdog stands for peace and love!
Barkley stands for trees and fun!
Ben stands for line and colour!

www.Speakerdog.com
www.BenTheIllustrator.com

Your cut-out and keep **Speakerdog!**

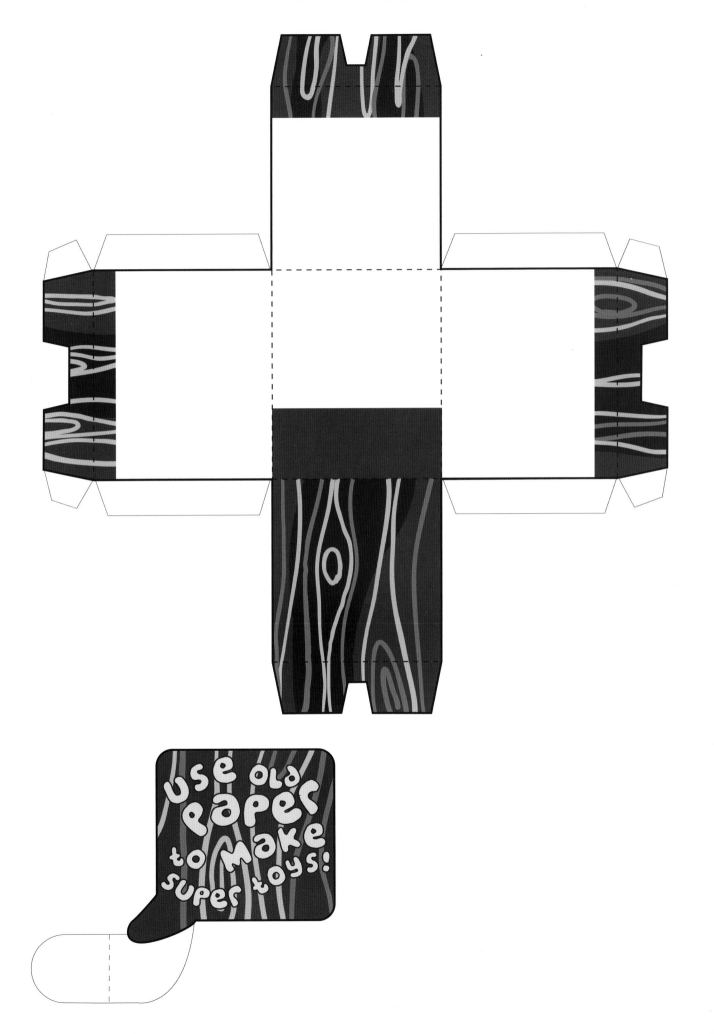

No. 19 **ROMMY**

by Tetsuya Watabe
Chiba, Japan

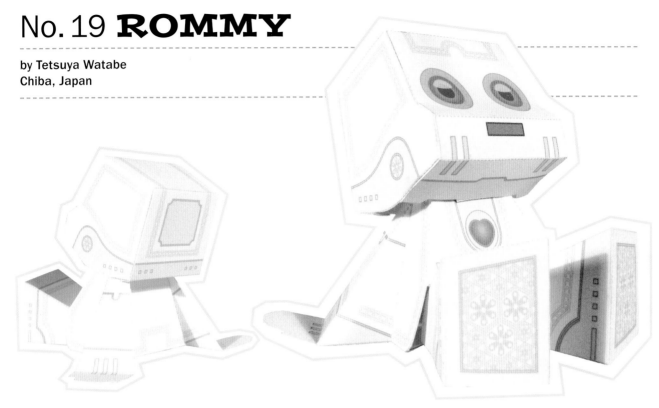

What was it that first inspired you to create your paper kits?

I have made models with plastics and metals previously. When I made it, my room was a mess of cutting scraps. I wanted to make models with easily handled materials and simple tools. I thought that it was paper. I made a penguin form with some color papers first. I had a great interest in the texture of the paper.

I made some models. And I thought if you can make well-planned patterns and intelligible instructions, anyone can build your forms. So I designed some paper kits.

What is the most challenging part of designing with paper?

It is important for me to build the attractive form that took in the character of paper. The 3-D form made with paper has some cut lines or fold lines. I aim at the lines to get a natural position for the form.

How long have you been making these wonderful paper kits?

I designed the first paper kit for a sale in 2005. I make two or three types a year.

Do you have a favorite paper kit you've designed?

The first kit was a pig sitting down holding a card. I think that the pig was successful because it had a very charming shape.

What was your inspiration for the Rommy project?

At first, I drew a robot on my sketchbook. It was a small robot that looked helpless and useless. I got the idea of this project from vinyl toys that one form has various graphic patterns. I thought that project was suitable for paper. Most vinyl toys look cool, fashionable and lovely. But I wanted to add a little spice of loneliness, sadness and melancholy to their original style.

Why did you decide to make Rommy a free project to download instead of a kit to purchase?

Because my paper kits are slightly small, I think it is difficult to build them for paper craft beginners. I want people to practice building an easy kit before building my kits. Beginners have better luck building a downloaded kit because they can print it again if they fail in building it.

As another reason, I wanted people all over the world to be able to build my kit.

How do you go about designing a new paper project?

First, I draw some rough sketches. Then I alternate between working on the computer and working with my hands.

What advice would you give people who want to design their own papertoys?

You can begin paper crafts with simple tools right now. Any way you can, try to cut a paper, hold a paper and paste a paper. If you don't like your finished toy, repeat the process. You should start something simple and increase your skills little by little.

No. 20 3EYEDBEAR

by Maarten Janssens
Amsterdam, The Netherlands

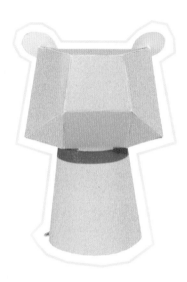

What was your inspiration for the 3EyedBear papertoy?

As an indoor kid (Dutch weather), I always was very crafty. And an image geek as well. I loved pop-ups and did a lot of that. But it gradually got replaced by hormones, girlfriends, music, school and eventually by getting a grip on my work as a comics illustrator. When I accidentally stumbled upon the work of Keisuke Saka a couple of years ago, all that sweet childhood fantasy came back like lightning, and I started researching the whole world of paper craft intensely. Toylava made me want to build my own kits. I love what they do. Their kits are so accessible; anyone should be able to build them within a reasonable amount of time. Sure, I hugely respect the ingeniously complicated paper craft of some engineers building castles, carrier ships or realistic motorcycles, but building a little character in half an hour—to me, that's magic. With the Pictoplasma thing happening, a lot of good stuff can be found out there nowadays. It's great and inspiring to see Shin Tanaka work like a fashion designer or the nifty stuff Readymech does. And you brought animation design into the game, not only in looks, but in movement, too. And I feel it's only the beginning of a big wave.

How the bear got about was actually quite simple. At the time, I was staying in Berlin with a colleague and when I asked him for a name for the web site, he said "three-eyed bear." It sounded so original that it had to work. That became the first kit, although the website itself took about two years before it launched.

So was 3EyedBear your first attempt at making a papertoy?

3EyedBear was indeed my own first paper kit. I had been building about fifty paper kits in the couple of months before, and the space on my bookshelves became occupied with little creatures. I did all the fast little stuff, from the BJ-Town landscapes and science kits Canon published, via the cars of Boooon, animals from Yamaha, some funny Flying Pig and brilliant Keisuke Saka kits and Toylava at Lexmark, all the way to models designed by then-new Pepakura software (I almost always hate them). By the time I designed the bear, I kind of knew how it worked and what I liked, but it took three re-designs before the kit got completed. It was tricky to estimate volumes on a flat design. It still is.

Do you have any sage advice for people who might be thinking about making their own papertoys?

The only real advice I can think of is to start simple, with one or two shapes together, maybe even "inspired" by existing models. But like everything, it comes down to just starting and doing it; it's rewarding and fun.

You have several different papertoys on your site, www.3EyedBear.com. Which one is the most popular?

My dream is to create a little world of characters, maybe and hopefully connected emotionally together in an environment. That's a long way from where I'm at: just doodling around and getting acquainted with the material. There are so many good one-model projects that I'm not even going to try to fit in. Besides that, I'm doing this for fun, so there's no reason to do it other than to please myself. I have the feeling the custom models are a bit of a "boys" thing, where I probably am pleasing the girls. In that theory, I don't think it's strange the Golddiggers get the most response, because they are, um, cute? I've worked for Disney for twelve years, so I kind of know my way around cuteness. The bear also gets a lot of positive response, but I guess it's too small for customizing, and too bold to be really cute. I still hope he will flourish someday, because it's obviously a precious one for me.

I think one of the more unique papertoys on your site is the e-cakes. Can you tell us a little about your e-cakes paper kit?

The e-cakes are my version of e-cards: just send someone 3-D love, or hate. I have a huge list here with wishes to produce and visualize, but I've really missed the opportunity (time, in fact) to do something with it so far. Unfortunately, plans keep on piling up faster than I can execute properly. I figured to shoot with a shotgun in open air first in hoping to find a connection with my audience before going into sniper mode. The e-cakes are one of those shots, but honestly, it's meant to be a huge series in the end. On the more earthly side, the e-cakes came as an idea after I visited the Calligraffiti show by Niels Shoe Meulman here

in Amsterdam. It made me want to explore the visual side of writing again. The cakes were supposed to be nice little canvases for me to be experimenting with that.

What advantage do you think paper has over toys made of vinyl or plush?

The material is hugely different. Paper is delicate, which I find very attractive, but it's also available everywhere. And it's cheap. Anyone can design a paper kit within a weekend and put it online for worldwide downloading on Monday. It's not that I don't like the vinyl toys, I love them, but I prefer its paper nephew, since all of us have access into that world and can influence its appearance. You could say it's more democratic.

What do you see in the future for papertoys?

Oh, I don't look into the future, but since papertoys seem to have all the stars aligned at the moment, it will stick to the Internet like glue for a while. At least, it's what I hope for, because I'm having a blast reliving parts of my childhood.

---

1. Prescore all dotted fold lines by gently running a craft knife down a straight edge.

2. Cut out all objects. Be sure to cut around the green line on the gold button on BODY and around the solid outline on the EARS.

3. Fold and glue tabs in numerical order.

4. Fold FEET out.

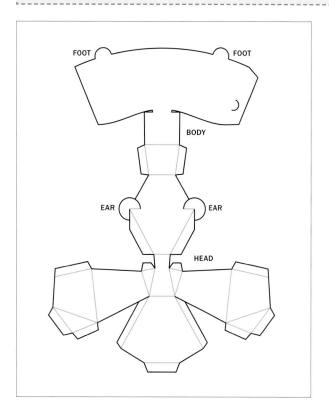

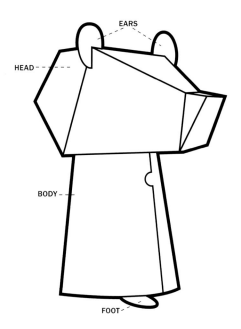

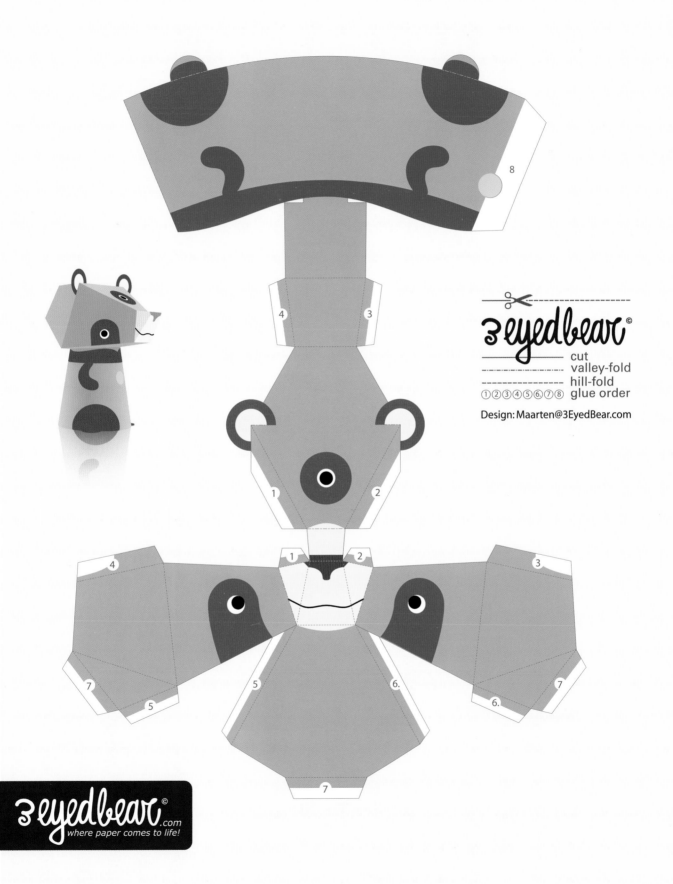

3eyedbear©
- - - - - cut
- - - - - valley-fold
- - - - - hill-fold
①②③④⑤⑥⑦⑧ glue order

Design: Maarten@3EyedBear.com

3eyedbear©.com
where paper comes to life!

No. 21 ANTLOR SECURITY

by Kenn Munk
Århus, Denmark

What inspired the Antlor project? Why did you decide to execute it as a paper kit?

I came up with Antlor—The Deer Departed in a pub with some other toy people: Aidan and Jon from Playlounge, a girl called Bridge, Matt Jones and Neil O'Rourke, who wrote for *Clutter* at the time. I rarely get useful ideas when drunk, but as we downed our Stellas and chatted about toys, this idea exploded in my mind—fully realized. After having won in the UK Design-A-Qee series back in ... hmm, was that 2004? ... I wanted to take things further, I wanted to design my own shape. And after asking around, vinyl or hard plastic would be too expensive, time-consuming and complicated for me, so I went with what I knew and made it in paper.

Had you done any dimensional paper work before?

I worked in advertising then, and I'd made loads of cardboard displays. Figuring out how things would fold and behave had sort of become one of my specialties at the agency, so that helped things. Before that, I had made cardboard models of our BMX bikes for me and the kids on my street back in the eighties.

Antlor is available in a lot of designer toy stores. How was Antlor received by the traditionally vinyl toy crowd?

To be honest, not very well. The vinyl toy crowd wants arms and legs. They want inanimate objects turned into creatures, they don't seem to want creatures turned into inanimate objects. So the place these sell best is actually design stores, quirky interior decoration places and such. The Antlor have a few devoted followers that really seem to like them, and that warms my heart.

Do you think people are a little intimidated about putting paper kits together? They might pay good money for them, then screw it up trying to put it together.

No, I don't think people are scared, even if they are likely to make a mess. I think the fact that they're dealing with paper helps. Regardless of the cost, once they're home with the kit and their scissors and glue, the kits are just paper, not gold leaf or expensive plastic. The people who buy my Antlor kits usually aren't people who built loads of model kits in their youth; they buy it for the idea and the quirkiness, and I estimate that most of my kits have never actually been built. This is probably also due to the fact that I deliberately designed them to be interesting objects when they're in their flat state.

Yeah, I love the way these look when they're flat. A lot of papertoys are really boxy. Your kits, on the other hand, have some cool graceful curves in them, and I really dig the inset eyes. Could you tell us a little about the process you used to design the Antlor series?

Thank you. Mine are quite boxy as well, most of the boxes just aren't rectangular. I think it helped that I hadn't seen any "designer" papertoys when I made them. After I'd released them, Brickboy sent me an e-mail saying that I wasn't alone. I have no idea which or how many papertoys were out there when I made these in 2004–2005, so there wasn't a style or set of unwritten rules that guided my thinking. I come from a background in advertising, so the shapes came from many, many hours designing store displays. The thinner paper allowed me to use curves that I couldn't have used with corrugated cardboard, so I took advantage of that. Everything you see on an Antlor sheet is made in Illustrator, no 3-D or Pepakura. It all had to be something I made, not something a computer calculated for me. Funny story about the eyes: I'd planned for two versions, "innies" (dead holes) and "outies" (bulging eyeballs), but in the end, the eyeballs seemed too silly. And they'd taken up space on my sheets that I'd rather use to make the kits as big as possible.

About how long did it take you to settle on the final designs?

When I woke up after that trip to the pub, I started sketching. I knew they'd be stylized, but at first they were more antler-like. I realized that I had to simplify them quite a bit, both for my own sanity and that of the poor people who'd build them. When I'd found a style, I worked from keywords to make them distinct; each one would have a defining feature, like "curved" or "wide." I got the idea in December, they hit the streets on April 1. So three months from alcohol-fueled idea to zip-lock-bagged product.

What are you up to now? Any new projects coming along, paper or otherwise?

Project-wise, I'm slowly squeezing Antlor series two into the world. The kit included in this book is the first design. It's currently called Antlor Security and is a surveillance-camera twist on series one.

I'm not going to print and release this like the original Antlor series. I want it to live off something else. It will pop up every now and again in magazines, as downloads and whatever. It's part of the whole secret surveillance-camera thing. Apart from that, I'm backing away from the toy thing a bit. I'm saddened by what is considered "good" in these circles. I'm trying to run my little business and make a living doing whatever takes my fancy.

---

1. Prescore all dotted fold lines by gently running a craft knife down a straight edge.

2. Cut out all objects. Be sure to cut out the crosses for the wires to go in.

3. Fold COWLING following the folding key.

4. Fold and glue MAIN BODY, ARM, JOINT and WIRE BOX.

5. Assemble LENS according to diagram.

6. Fold and glue PLAQUE and HANGING BAR. Glue HANGING BAR to back of PLAQUE.

7. Glue pieces together as marked.

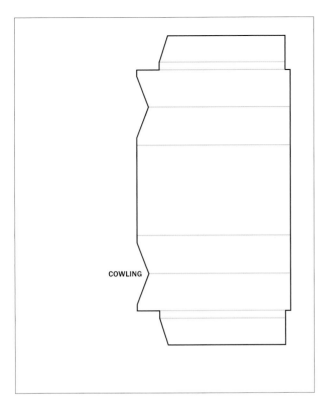

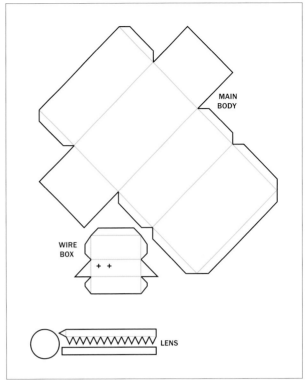

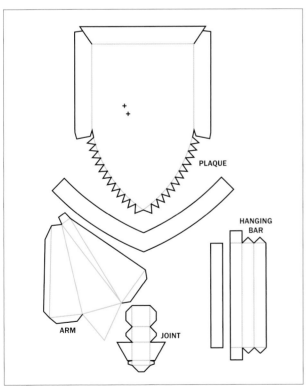

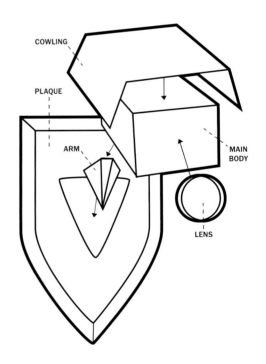

security

2

8411

FRONT

this object is:
COWLING ➡

WIRING
your security:

use two pieces of black wire or string.

make little holes in:

attach one end of each wire to WIREBOX.

attach other end of each wire to PLAQUE.

switch on and watch thy neighbour.

8411

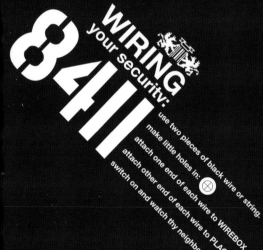

8411

securitv
WATCH CRAFT:

——————— means "CUT"

·············· means "SCORE + FOLD: ⬦ "

·············· means "SCORE + FOLD: ⬦ "

——————— means "GLUE"

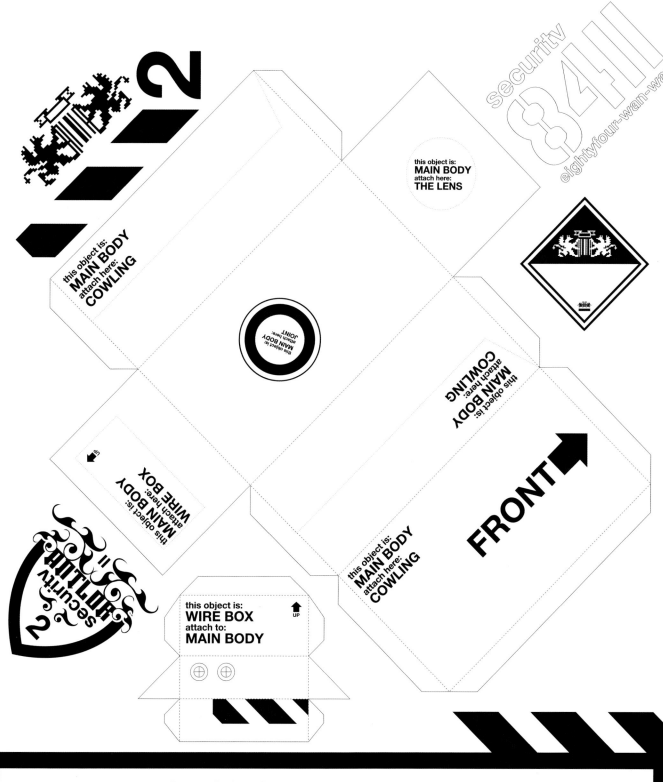

2

this object is:
MAIN BODY
attach here:
THE LENS

this object is:
MAIN BODY
attach here:
COWLING

this object is:
MAIN BODY
attach here:
JOINT

this object is:
MAIN BODY
attach here:
COWLING

this object is:
MAIN BODY
attach here:
WIRE BOX

FRONT ➤

security
BUTLER
2

this object is:
WIRE BOX
attach to:
MAIN BODY
↑ UP

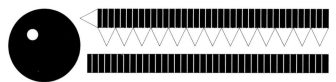

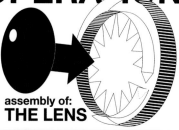

WARNING: SECURITV IN OPERATION

◀ these objects are:
THE LENS
attach to:
MAIN BODY

assembly of:
THE LENS

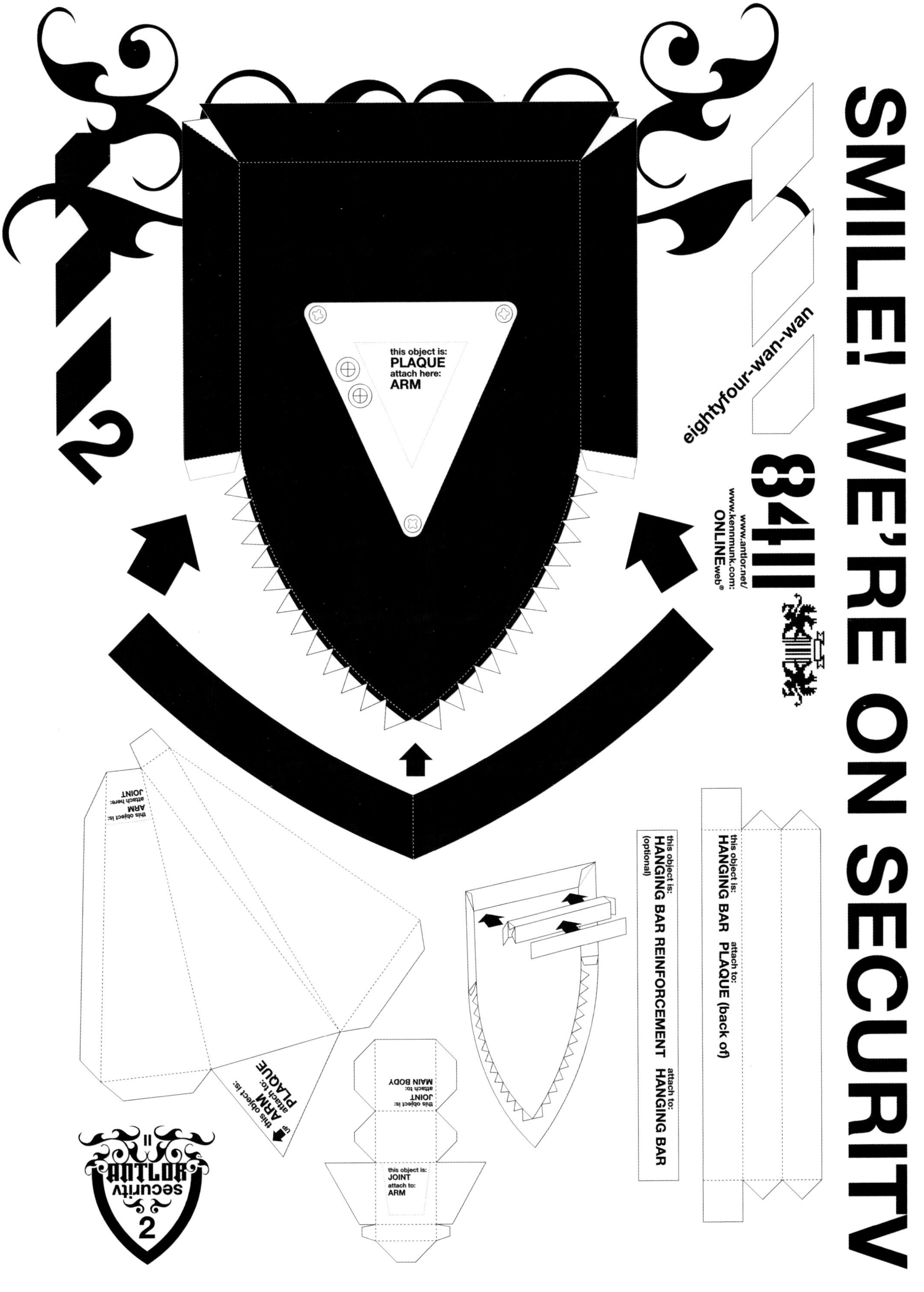

SMILE! WE'RE ON SECURITY

eightyfour-wan-wan

8411

www.antlor.net/
www.kennmunk.com:
ONLINEweb®

this object is:
PLAQUE
attach here:
ARM

this object is:
ARM
attach here:
JOINT

this object is:
ARM
attach to:
PLAQUE

this object is:
JOINT
attach to:
MAIN BODY

this object is:
JOINT
attach to:
ARM

this object is:
HANGING BAR
attach to:
PLAQUE (back of)

this object is:
HANGING BAR REINFORCEMENT
(optional)
attach to:
HANGING BAR

ANTLOR
security
2

2

No. 22 CRIMINAL TOY

by Carlo Giovani
São Paulo, Brazil

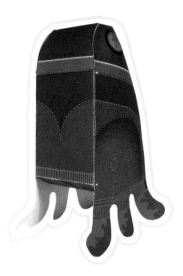

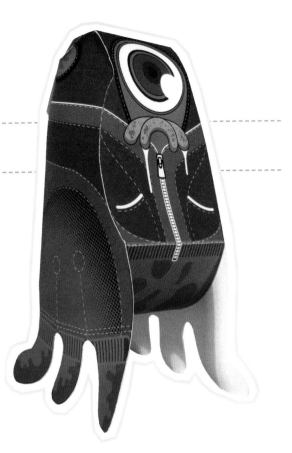

How did you get started designing with paper?

I started in Federal University of Santa Maria, [Brazil], in the graphic design course.

What are some of the advantages of paper over other mediums?

I think paper is a cheap material compared with some others, with great versatility and a lot of different textures, colors and sizes. You can adapt paper for any kind of project, from toys to roofs.

What do you see that is more challenging about paper as a medium?

The industrial process, making a collection of toys or packs with complex knives, special colors and formats. To make it happen as you designed it is challenging.

Can you give us a little insight into how you go about designing one of your projects?

I start with some sketches, and after that, I make some prototypes, modeling the paper as a very organic structure. So I never start by using mathematic methods. When the prototype is ready, I make some corrections on the computer, and it's done and ready to be printed. I don't use 3-D programs in the process.

What are some of the coolest projects you've done lately?

The Criminal Toys, the Nação Zumbi masks and the Turbo Trio disc cover are some of the greatest works that we have done in

Carlo Giovani Studio last year. There are four more people who help me with the projects here at the studio.

Until 2004 I worked alone. Since that year, the structure grew up and now I'm a kind of art director here. We have a lot of projects at the same time and nowadays it's necessary to have a team to take care of all the jobs.

I love your stop-motion paper work. Do you feel that paper lends itself well to animation? What are some of the unique challenges you find animating with paper?

Paper is a very interesting media to work with on stop-motion animation because you can develop your own method or style. You don't have a lot of references to create limits in your work, so you can adapt, make some freestyles. The most difficult part on it is the articulations. They are very fragile structures.

What was your inspiration for the Criminal Toys series?

Japan monsters or sentais, like Spectroman, sci-fi B-movies and that kind of thrash-classic thing.

It seems like tons of designer papertoys are popping up lately. What makes yours unique?

Each designer has their own references, their experiences and work process. Those particularities make their works unique.

How do you think papertoys are viewed by most folks? Do you think that because the medium is paper instead of vinyl or

plush that papertoys seem somehow less valuable? Could they ever be viewed as equals?

Yes, I think papertoys are different than vinyl, plush, even wood toys. We need to consider the production costs, the durability, etc. Of course, there is the artistic value, so if Takashi Murakami produced his own papertoy, it would cost a thousand dollars.

What advice would you give to someone who wants to get in on the paper game?

Be patient, trust in your ideas and have great persistence.

---

1. Prescore all dotted fold lines by gently running a craft knife down a straight edge. Score the curved dashed lines on the front of character freehand.

2. Glue notches in top of sides together.

3. Pinch the curved folds on the front to form folds.

4. Glue tabs on top of HEAD to the inside of the sides of head so that the white marks line up with the folds.

5. Gently curve the bottom of the front panel to form the underside.

6. Glue back panel in place, matching up the white arrows to the folds.

7. Curve the TENTACLES outward.

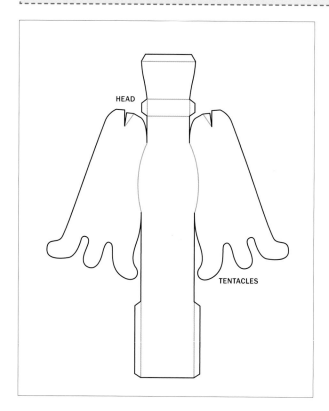

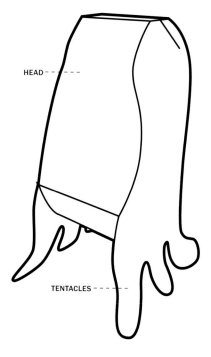

No. 23 KRAMPUS SQUEALER

by Christopher Bonnette
Los Angeles, California, USA

What was it that inspired you to start making papertoys?

A Cub Scout leader introduced me to origami at age seven by making a flapping paper crane. I carefully deconstructed it and refolded it over and over again. Finally, I learned how to make it on my own. Soon I began to go to the library and get every origami book I could find. My mother was very crafty and my father is technical, which is a good combination for a paper engineer. They were happy that I had a quiet hobby, so they continued to nurture it. I started with origami, but soon found other books on paper crafts. I still have most of my first books that started this fascinating hobby and career, some dating back to the early eighties. My hope is to continue further developing my skills in paper engineering for the enjoyment of others.

As someone who has been into origami and paper crafting for a while, what do you think of the current trend of designer and urban papertoys?

I think the trend of the designer and urban papertoys scene is great. Most artists don't get much of a break. I myself tried really hard to break into the vinyl toy scene. I asked a lot of questions and did all kinds of research. It all boiled down to "if you are not an already known profitable artist, then we won't work with you." With papertoys, it just takes a little time, ink and paper, and you have yourself a custom original toy. I think I actually like papertoys better than vinyl because they are more like model kits and you have a hand in building them yourself. Papertoys have really caught on thanks to the Internet. All kinds of artists and designers with like minds from all over the world

are having so much fun swapping templates and making new custom papertoys. It is very nice to see people taking their time to build one of your creations, and being so proud they made it themselves that they have to share it with all of their friends.

I love the mouths on your Squealer papertoy—it's almost puppet-like. What was your inspiration for the Squealer project?

Many different things inspired me in the design of the Squealer papertoy. I researched and looked at many other designers' vinyl and papertoys because I wanted to make something different. I knew I did not want the head to be square, so I started from there and sketched many different shapes until I came up with the final version. The body is a relatively simple trapezoid, which makes for a nice body shape. The arms are triangular-shaped, with round, mitten-like hands. I thought it was a nice ice-cream-cone shape that many people would find cute. I definitely had a moving mouth in mind from the beginning. I have a few themes that appear in many of my illustrations, and big mouths with many teeth is one of them, so I had to add that. I wanted to create a papertoy that was well thought out in construction so many people could build it without too much difficulty.

I always wanted to create a papertoy but never got around to making one until I joined the Stylus website (http://styl.us). It is a collective and collaborative art blog and forum created by Ray Frenden. Ray and I, along with many other talented artists, got to talking, and I volunteered to design a papertoy template. And that is how the Squealer project was born.

A lot of your paper toys and art are based around mythology and folklore. Can you tell us a little about your fascination with these topics?

I have always loved tall tales. I have collected many books on mythology and folklore from all around the world. The one thing I noticed was that most of the books did not have pictures, and if they did, they were very old. I want to update the pictorial history of the creatures of legend. I try to create the illustrations as accurately as possible, but still keep them whimsical, stylish and modern. If the image is not fully accurate to its original description, I will state it as an artist's interpretation. I have also been lucky enough to make new friends due to this illustration project. Richard Freeman, a real cryptozoologist, came across the web site, and we have become friends. He

is part of the Centre for Fortean Zoology. With his help and knowledge, I try to get the facts on odd creatures as accurate as possible. No one truly knows how these creatures may have looked. I am dedicated to keeping the tales of the past known so they are not forgotten. I still hold the hope that mankind has a lot left to discover.

What advice would you give to people who want to design their own paper toys?

Always sketch it out first. Do what makes you happy. Make sure you are having fun. Take your time. Adobe Illustrator, a see-through ruler with a grid, and sharp craft knife blades are essential.

1. Prescore all fold lines by gently running a craft knife down a straight edge.

2. Cut out all objects. Be sure to cut bottom of fangs and around the outside of the ears and slots in HANDS.

3. Fold and glue fronts to backs on TAIL, BAD CHILD, SWITCH and FORK.

4. Glue BODY together and glue tab between MOUTH and BODY to bottom of MOUTH so MOUTH protrudes from BODY.

5. Fold and glue ARMS.

6. Fold and glue HEAD tabs around from attached side.

7. Glue ARMS onto sides of BODY and TAIL to back of BODY.

8. Glue TONGUE inside MOUTH.

9. Insert FORK and SWITCH into HANDS.

10. Fold and glue BASKET and glue to back of BODY.

11. Place BAD CHILD inside BASKET.

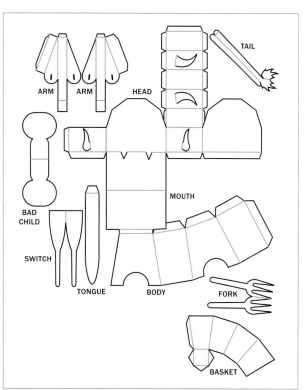

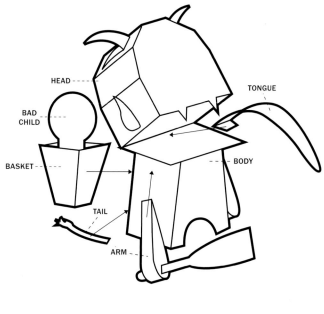

Arm   Arm

Tail

Bad Child

Head Front   Head Back

Tongue

Mouth Inside Top

Mouth Inside Bottom

Switch

Body Back

Body Front

©2007 www.macula.tv

Fork

Basket Backpack

No. 24 GHOSTBOY

by Sharim Gubbels
Tilburg, The Netherlands

What inspired you to start making papertoys?

Well, I had always been into character design, but wanted to move away from 2-D to create something tangible. Designer toys held my interest, but I disliked the limitations of vinyl. I also wanted to create something that would allow for easy interaction and collaboration with other designers. Paper seemed perfect and allowed for mistakes and experimentation. At that time, [designer] papertoys weren't really around all that much, or at least compared to nowadays. However, I loved the almost overly intricate Japanese mech paper craft models based on certain animes—complete with moving joints. Their setup was way too complicated and time-consuming for my taste and plans, but they did inspire me to create my own personal world of mechs, vehicles and their drivers.

What was the first papertoy you designed?

Hmm, let me think. I guess it was the mini Worker character in combination with the Sparkplug mech. I had been playing around with different shapes of paper blocks for a bit and had sketched out some ideas I had for the mech, keeping in mind what kind of parts I'd need for that and how much time it would take to build. After that, I just started creating the parts one by one in Photoshop by trial and error until I was satisfied. And presto chango, I ended up with my first Crossville papertoy.

Can you tell us a little about your papertoy world Crossville and what it's all about?

Crossville and its name came to be because of two main reasons, I guess. One, it would provide a perfect place for me to cross over from 2-D to 3-D, as well as a fun place to cross over with other artists, something I enjoy a lot and that is always an extra incentive to keep going. The other reason is that I didn't want to randomly create toys, so I decided on having all my creations be a part of this one contained world, from its inhabitants to their vehicles and mechs, or even foliage. It adds an extra dimension to the creation process, which keeps it interesting to me, and it's fun to see the world expanding over time. Hopefully it will keep doing so.

Was making the leap from 2-D to 3-D hard? What effect has your 3-D work had on your 2-D work?

I wouldn't say it was that hard, actually. I've always loved trying to figure out how things work and fit, the only difference being that normally it would end up as a 2-D graphic. But, of course, it took me—and, every now and then, it will still take me—a few tries to get more complicated shapes figured out. As far as any effects on my 2-D work, I don't think there have been any.

Do you ever sell your toys or make them available to download?

There were plans to do so when I first started out. But El Carmesi and Sparkplug ended up being too intricate to get a nice flow of designs in, as well as probably proving too much of a pain to build at home. With the new Ghostboy—the first to be spawned from the decays of the older Crossville mechs—it might all change.

Can you tell us a little bit about your process for creating a new paper model for Crossville?

They all have to make sense within that world. So after a basic idea on what kind of a model (shape and style-wise) I'd like to create, and how that would fit into the big picture, I'll get to scribbling and sketching. The next step is simply deconstructing it into paper "blocks," if you will, and creating them, usually first in Photoshop. And that's pretty much it.

What do you find most alluring about paper as a medium?

The versatility of it. Paper can have completely different characteristics when applied in various ways. The outcome can very much retain a paper "look," but when constructed differently, it can also have a very solid-looking outcome, almost masking the fact that it's paper. Using papers of a different thickness also allows for a variety of very strong, hard shapes, as well as pliable ones. The only limitation is your mind, basically. And time, of course. An added bonus is the easy way of sharing the templates for collaboration, as well as being able to just print it out and build it, no mass production necessary if you don't want to.

What advice would you give people who want to design their own papertoys?

I'd say play around for a bit first—shapes, sizes, curves, edges, the "weight" of an object. That way, you can exactly create the vibe you want for each toy you create. Once you have that figured out, the sky is the limit!

---

1. Prescore all fold lines by gently running a craft knife down a straight edge.

2. Cut out all objects. Be sure to cut slots for ARMS and LEGS.

3. Glue LEGS and ARMS front to back.

4. Fold and glue HEAD.

5. Fold and glue NECK.

6. Glue NECK inside HEAD by gluing tabs on NECK to the underside of the top of HEAD. NECK should angle forward toward face.

7. Glue the FRONT and BACK of BODY OUTSIDE together with the black side out.

8. Glue BODY INSIDE together.

9. Glue BODY OUTSIDE around BODY INSIDE starting at the spot marked.

10. Insert ARMS and LEGS into slots on BODY.

11. Insert BODY into NECK.

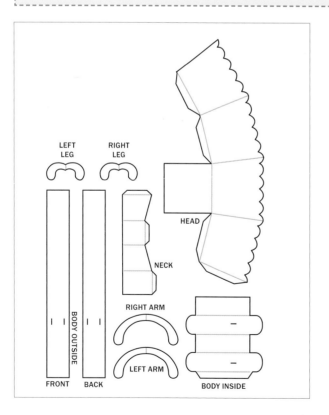

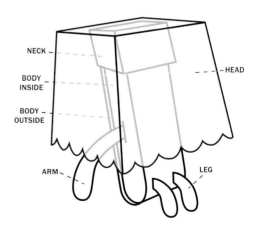

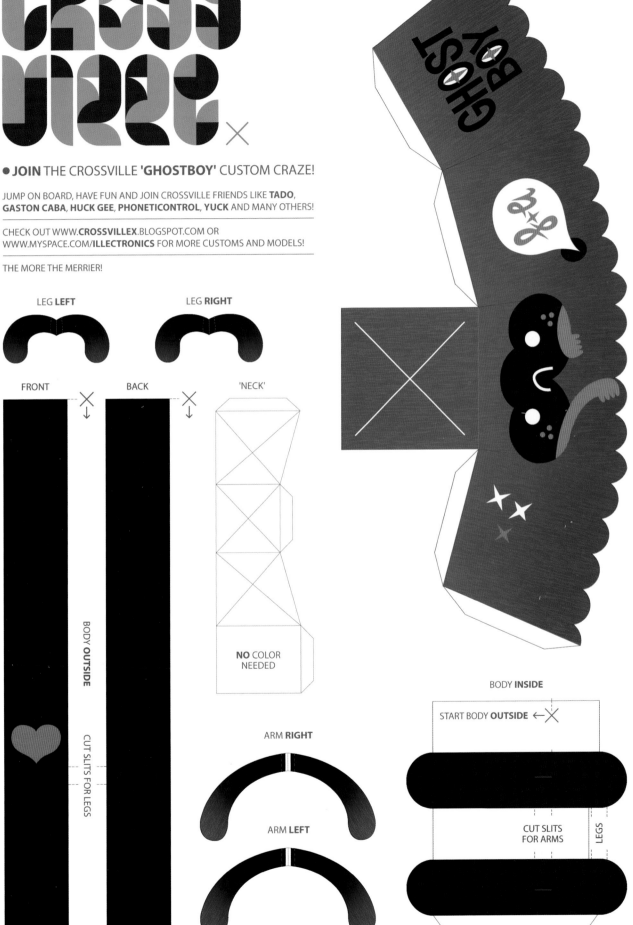

CROSS VILLE ✕

● **JOIN** THE CROSSVILLE **'GHOSTBOY'** CUSTOM CRAZE!

JUMP ON BOARD, HAVE FUN AND JOIN CROSSVILLE FRIENDS LIKE **TADO**, **GASTON CABA**, **HUCK GEE**, **PHONETICONTROL**, **YUCK** AND MANY OTHERS!

CHECK OUT WWW.**CROSSVILLE**X.BLOGSPOT.COM OR WWW.MYSPACE.COM/**ILLECTRONICS** FOR MORE CUSTOMS AND MODELS!

THE MORE THE MERRIER!

LEG **LEFT**

LEG **RIGHT**

FRONT

BACK

'NECK'

NO COLOR NEEDED

BODY **OUTSIDE**

CUT SLITS FOR LEGS

HEAD **FRONT**

GHOST BOY

ARM **RIGHT**

ARM **LEFT**

BODY **INSIDE**

START BODY **OUTSIDE** ←✕

CUT SLITS FOR ARMS

LEGS

No. 25 SON OF A GRUMM

by Matthijs Kamstra, a.k.a. [mck]
Amsterdam, The Netherlands

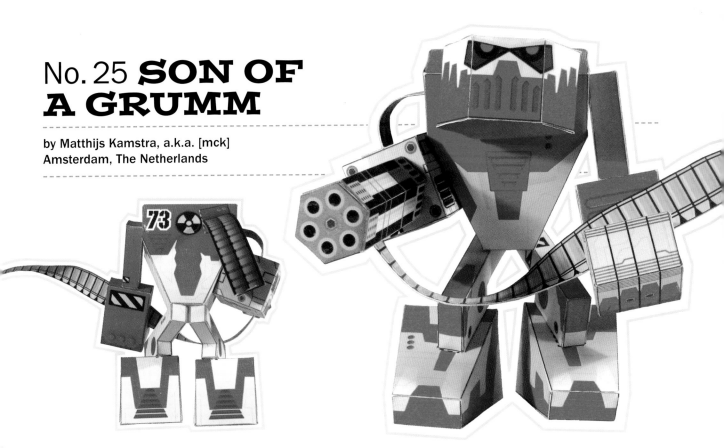

What first got you interested in papertoys?

The first time I came into contact with papertoys was when I read a magazine called *Reload*. In it was an article about designer toys. One of them was a cool baseball figure called Brickboy. After some Internet research, I quickly found out that Brickboy was designed by Sjors Trimbach, and that it was possible to download, print and make different custom designs of Brickboy. And, of course, that it was totally free. After building a couple of models, I put in some more hours looking for other people involved in this thing. Naturally, I found the many free models of airplanes, ships and cars, but also people who made Gundam, manga and anime models. When I discovered Shin Tanaka, I immediately knew I wanted to make a papertoy, too, and that's when I created Grumm.

What was it about Shin's work that struck you?

By that time, he was one of the few people who I could find on the 'net who was busy with urban paper craft.

The models he made at that time—the first time I stumbled upon Shin's work, he was doing the Spiky Baby (series 3) and Gritty—immediately appealed to me! This probably had to do with his love for sneakers, Michael Lau and his graffiti background. I happen to share all three of those with him.

However, I am the most impressed by the way he creates his models with flowing lines without making his cutouts too complicated. To me, the best example still is Gritty. This model can be printed on one piece of paper, it's easy to build, and when you

make it, you have got a paper craft model with an attitude. By using some sort of hood, the model's got two faces! To me, Gritty is an example of paper craft that easily competes with vinyl toys.

What's also special to me is that Shin managed to create very simple paper models that are customized by a lot of designers and are put online for a limited amount of time in which they can be downloaded, so they become collectibles. That makes it quite difficult to obtain a Spiky Baby from the old series.

It's cool how Shin uses some stuff out of the vinyl toy playbook for his papertoys. Can you tell us a little about the process you went through to design Grumm?

After seeing and building a couple of paper craft models, I wanted to create one myself.

First, I made up a list with requirements for my model:

1. It had to fit on an A4-size piece of paper.
2. It had to look cool.
3. It had to consist of easy shapes.
4. There should be no curved lines.
5. There should be enough room to make an illustration.

After this, I created a few drafts, and then I started building a prototype. This first prototype I quickly put together with cardboard and tape, but it gave me the feeling I was on the right track. I cut the model apart, flattened it (where possible), scanned it and copied it in Illustrator. Using Illustrator, I gave depth to the parts that were flat. Then I printed it and rebuilt it.

During the building of the model, I checked if the glue tabs were at the correct and most useful spots, and after the model was ready, I checked if the proportions were right. I thought the legs were too thick, so I went back to Illustrator, implemented all the modifications, printed it again and built my third prototype.

Now Grumm was ready to be colored, and this became Grumm the Screamer Red. However, I made one concession: Grumm can be printed on one page, but I prefer printing him on two pages. I have captured this process in detail, and you can read all about it on my blog (www.matthijskamstra.nl/blog).

How did you decide on the name "Grumm"?

I would like to be able to say I came up with the name Grumm, but I can't. A friend of mine, Enkeling, did, based on one of my first sketches. It's a combination of grumpy, grim and [the Brothers] Grimm.

What advice would you give to people who want to create their own papertoys?

Keep it simple! I know you can create stupid fresh shit with 3-D programs and Pepakura Designer, but they're often very hard to build. And if you aren't familiar with these programs, it'll cost you a whole lot of time to learn them. However, you can work wonders with simple 3-D forms. It's a bit like drawing; everything is reducible to geometric shapes, such as a square, circle and triangle. This also applies to papertoys, but here the geometric forms are 3-D: cubes, cylinders, tubes and cones. Using adaptations of these forms, almost everything is possible.

Can you tell us a little about what you do when you're not working on Grumm?

I work for an advertising and marketing company as a designer/animator/programmer/and-some-other-stuff. My specialty is Flash, both animation/motion design and programming. Apart from that, I have to teach my less-experienced colleagues the ins and outs.

Outside of my work, I spend a lot of time behind my computer, too, working on my blog, creating visual experiments with Flash, coming up with paper models. And I surf the 'net. To me, the 'net is much better than a book or television. But I believe in balance, so I sport three evenings a week.

What are some of your other interests?

Mostly these two things: street art and computer art, in the broadest sense possible.

A list of keywords might help: street art, graffiti, graphic design, toy design, stickers, web design, sneakers, street wear, hip-hop, tattoos, papertoys, vinyl toys, hip-hop culture, rap music, video games, pixel art, vector art, stencil art, science fiction, robots, manga, designer toys, paper craft, Flash, ActionScript 2, ActionScript 3, AS2, AS3, Adobe, urban paper craft, Pepakura, Mech,

Gundam, anime, animation, design, toys, Pencak Silat, K1, snowboards, stencils, urban art, T-shirts.

How do you stay inspired?

Simple: the Internet. Every time I think there's nothing new left under the sun, I find something that's super interesting.

What does the future hold for urban paper craft? What do you see being the next step in the evolution?

Before I start talking about the future, I will share my vision about what is happening right now. I see two groups in paper craft: the traditional paper craft and the urban paper craft. In traditional paper craft, the models are paper replicas of real objects, like cars, animals, anime characters, etc. These models are complex, printed on a couple pieces of paper (most of the time, more than three pages) and will take a couple of nights (or longer) to build. Because the model is a replica of something realistic, there is no need for more than one artwork ("skin"). The models are often so complex that it would be too difficult for another designer to create a custom skin for such a model.

Urban paper craft focuses on simple paper models, mostly paper character designs. The models are printed on one or two pieces of paper, are usually easy to build and can be put together in a couple of hours. Because the models are based upon basic 3-D forms (cubes, cylinders, tubes and cones), they have a boxy appearance. These simple 3-D shapes make it possible for another designer to create a custom skin. Not only the 3-D form of the model itself will make it attractive, but also the surface skin design.

I know I'm creating a very black-and-white picture. Of course, there are paper craft models that don't fit in either group I just described. But it helps me to figure out what I'm going to do with urban paper craft in the near future.

I think the success of an urban paper craft model depends on how easily it can be built, if it can be printed on one piece of paper, how many parts there are (less is better). And the overall look of the model should be organic.

Grumm is none of this, so how will I make Grumm attractive for designers? I'm creating expansion packs for Grumm: There is a basic template for Grumm, but you can choose different heads, hands, feet and other accessories. So you're not only creating a custom skin, you're also creating a custom Grumm. And I'm hoping that other designers will create expansion packs, too.

Another important thing for success is user participation. Yeah, I know, another Internet buzzword. But the 'net is the most important medium where we can show our paper craft models. So, besides having a site and a place to show and download the models you created yourself, there should always be a possibility for users to create their own designs on blank templates, and a way to show these custom creations on your site (everybody wants their fifteen minutes of fame), or even to download it so other people can build it themselves.

So what will be the next thing for urban paper craft?

Well, I'm going to focus on creating more organic models, models that are articulated. And I will use my Flash skills to make it easier for users to participate in either creating paper craft models or creating skins.

1. Prescore all fold lines by gently running a creaft knife down a straight edge.

2. Cut out all objects.

3. Fold and glue HEAD, ARM, LEGS, FEET, BODY, GUN and GUN BARREL.

4. Fold and glue AMMO BELT, BIG TUBE and LITTLE TUBE front to back, making sure not to glue tabs together on ends of TUBES and AMMO BELT.

5. Glue body parts together by matching up corresponding numbers.

6. Glue AMMO BELT to GUN BARREL and place in HAND.

7. Glue SMALL and BIG TUBES to GUN and BODY as shown on diagram on toy.

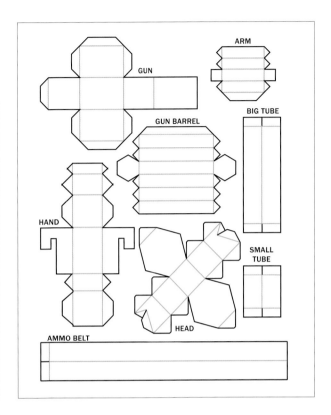

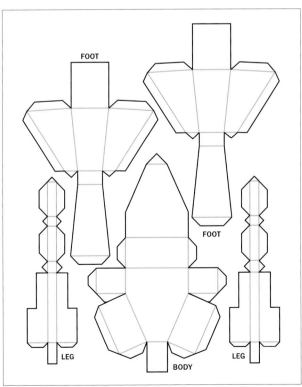

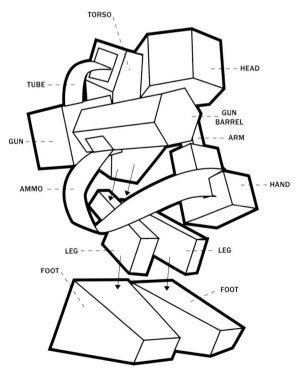

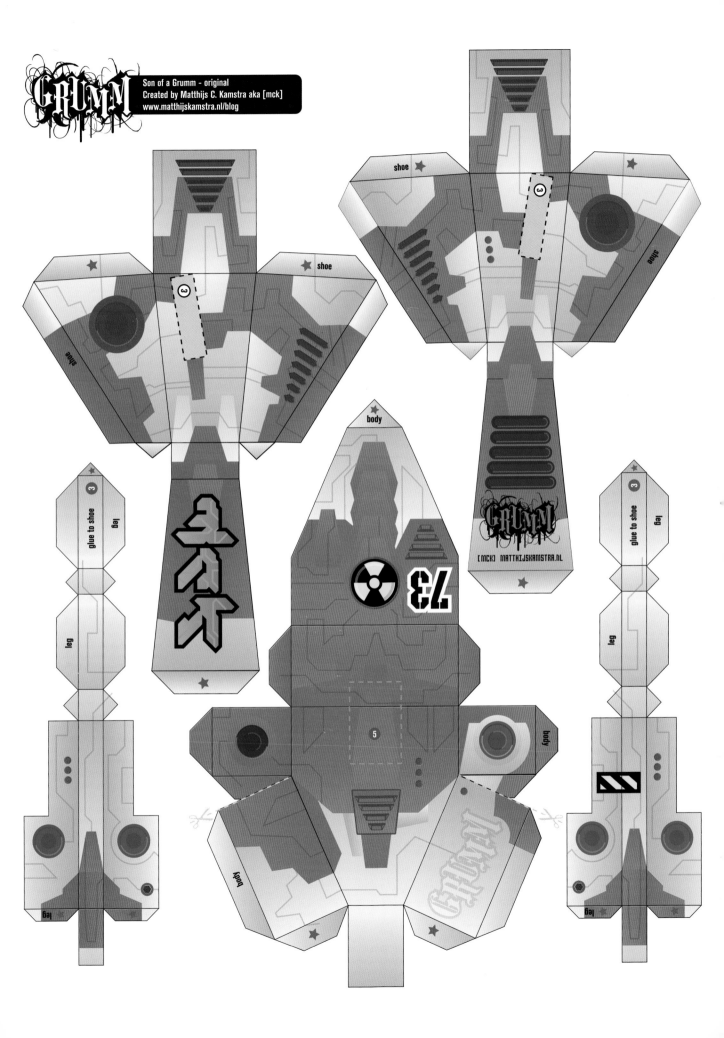

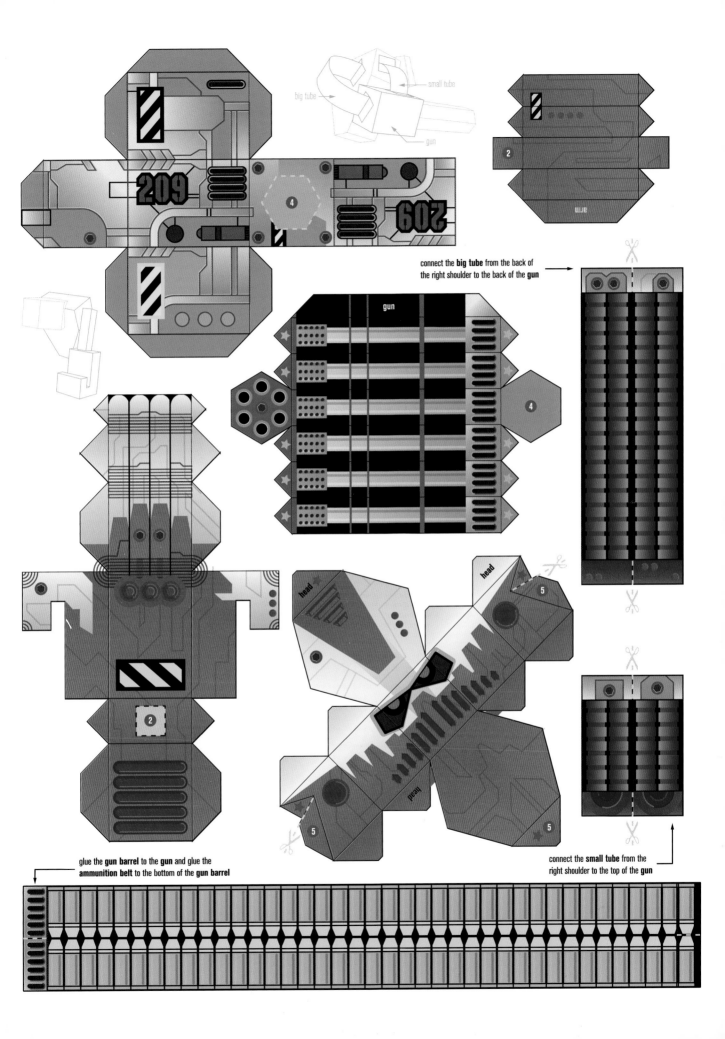

small tube

big tube

gun

209

209

4

connect the **big tube** from the back of the right shoulder to the back of the **gun**

gun

4

2

2

head

head

head

5

5

5

connect the **small tube** from the right shoulder to the top of the **gun**

glue the **gun barrel** to the **gun** and glue the **ammunition belt** to the bottom of the **gun barrel**

CONTRIBUTORS

3EYEDBEAR
Maarten Janssens
http://3eyedbear.com

**ANTLOR
SECURITV**
Kenn Munk
www.kennmunk.com

BARKLEY
Ben the Illustrator
www.speakerdog.com

BIGCHIEF TOY
BigChief Design
http://bigchief.it

BOXY
Shin Tanaka
http://shin.co.nr

BURLABOX
Atelier Alessio Blanco
http://burlabox.altervista.org

CRIMINAL TOY
Carlo Giovani
http://carlogiovani.com

E440
Ringo Krumbiegel
http://alle440.blog.com

FELTY BOY
Jerom
http://jerom-bd.blogspot.com/

FREAKY TIKI
Brian Castleforte
www.nicebunny.com

GHOSTBOY
Sharim Gubbels
www.illectronics.com

GO BANANAS
Horrorwood
http://horrorwood.info/blog

HOTROD DOGBUG
Sjors Trimbach
www.sjorstrimbach.com

**KRAMPUS
SQUEALER**
Christopher Bonnette
http://macula.tv

MAX 95
Jon Greenwell, a.k.a.
    Jonny Chiba
http://headnoddaz.
    blogspot.com

**MICRO
TOYPAPER**
Rememberthelittleguy
www.toypaper.co.uk

**NANIDAD AND
THE PEEPS**
mckibillo
www.nanibird.com

**NO ANCHOVIES
ANDY**
LouLou
www.loulouandtummie.com

OLIVER OLLIE
Matt Hawkins
www.custompapertoys.com

PAPERBOY
Marshall Alexander
www.marshallalexander.net

REDY
Angello García Bassi,
    a.k.a. Cubotoy
www.cubotoy.co.nr

ROMMY
Tetsuya Watabe
www.kamimodel.com

SIZZA
Nick Knite
www.nickknite.com

SON OF A GRUMM
Matthijs Kamstra, a.k.a. [mck]
www.matthijskamstra.nl/blog

THUG
Filippo Perin, a.k.a. PHIL
www.myspace.com/philtoys

UNIT.2
Bryan Rollins
http://youdontseeus.
    blogspot.com

MORE GREAT BOOKS
FROM HOW

COMPLETE COLOR INDEX

With over 2,600 color combinations, this box set is all you'll need for solutions to your color problems! It contains the original best-selling *Color Index* and *Color Index 2*, and together they comprise the most comprehensive color selection tool out there.

ISBN: 978-1-60061-333-3, two books in box, #Z2976

BEYOND TREND

The pressure is on for creative people to deliver the newest looks and ideas. You need to stay in front of the cutting edge for your clients. Let *Beyond Trend* teach you how to effectively absorb the world around you and figure out what's next.

ISBN: 978-1-58180-961-9, hardcover, 224 p, #Z0682

THE WEB DESIGNER'S IDEA BOOK

The Web Designer's Idea Book includes more than 700 websites arranged thematically so you can find inspiration of layout, color, style and more. It's a must-have for starting any new web projects.

ISBN: 978-1-60061-064-6, paperback, 250 p, #Z1756

WOMEN OF DESIGN

Even in the 21st century, gender still influences the graphic design industry. *Women of Design* celebrates the work of women designers—both industry veterans and influential newcomers.

ISBN: 978-1-60061-085-1, paperback, 244 p, #Z1946

These and other great HOW Books titles are available at your local bookstore, from online suppliers and at www.howbookstore.com

BOOKS

www.howdesign.com